# LEGENDS OF OLD WILMINGTON & CAPE FEAR

JOHN HIRCHAK

Charleston ‖H‖ London

THE
History
PRESS

Published by The History Press
Charleston, SC 29403
www.historypress.net

First published 2014

Manufactured in the United States

ISBN 978.1.62619.463.2

Library of Congress CIP data applied for.

*For my wife, Kim, and my mother, Anne,*
*the two most funny, intelligent and courageous women in my life.*

# CONTENTS

# CONTENTS

# ACKNOWLEDGEMENTS

This is only a partial list of the many people who helped make this book possible and to whom I owe a tremendous debt of gratitude.

I want to thank the incredible group of characters who perform the Ghost Walk of Old Wilmington, the Haunted Pub Crawl and the Hollywood Location Walk: Denise Ward, Mike Hartle, John Henry Scott, Tara Noland, Anthony Lawson, Stan Wood, Charles Auten, Jamey Stone, Holli Saperstein, Kitty Fitzgibbon, Michael Brady, Laurie Bianco, Deb Barbeln and Steve Gallian. Thank you for bringing these stories to life, night after night, through your incredible gift of storytelling. You are all true masters of the craft, and I am truly fortunate to be able to call you my friends.

Of equal importance, and without whom the time to write this book couldn't have been made possible, I need to thank the truly awesome gang at the Black Cat Shoppe and Jokilimi Island Imports: Margot Beberaggi, Gina Shields, Amanda Hamilton (who is also often on the front lines of the Ghost Walk and Pub Crawl), Sandy Johnson, Jennifer Robbins and Sidney Ridenhour. You are all incredibly talented, intelligent, wonderful people, and I thank all of you for being in my life.

I also owe a tremendous debt of gratitude not only to the families, business owners, volunteers and associates affiliated with the sites and locations mentioned in this book, but also to all the others who helped make this unusual path I am on possible. I would like to especially thank the Reichert family, the Wilmington Railroad Museum, Don Barlow and St. James Episcopal Church, Connie Nelson and the entire staff at the Wilmington and Beaches Convention & Visitor's Bureau.

Thank you to the incredible historians and researchers in the local history room at the New Hanover Public Library: Jennifer Daugherty, Joseph Sheppard and Beverly Tetterton (retired). You have helped steer me in the right direction for fifteen years. If there are any historical inaccuracies, it's your fault! All kidding aside, I promise you, the reader, that I make no claim to being a historian. If there are any historical errors, I am fully to blame, and I apologize. I am appreciative of all the guidance from the State Archives of North Carolina, the United States Library of Congress, NCPedia.org, the North Carolina History Project, North Carolina Historic Sites, the Lower Cape Fear Historical Society, the University of North Carolina–Wilmington, the University of North Carolina and the National Park Service.

I would also like to thank the fine folks at Darwin Brewery and Brewlab for helping keep me straight when it comes to beer and porter. I especially want to thank Dr. Keith Thomas, who was very giving of his time. The Original Flag Porter 1825 is sincerely one of the greatest brews I have ever tasted. Cheers!

I also need to thank the good people at The History Press for agreeing to publish this book. I would especially like to thank Banks Smither for giving me the latitude I needed in order to complete this task. Thank you for the much-needed extensions and for your patience throughout the writing process.

Thank you to Ed Feeley, John Feeley, Glen Kashin, Dave Kellogg, Mark Klein, Frank Kramer, Craig Simmons, Stuart Wilding and your families for your friendship, understanding, guidance and support. To Cristobal Feeley, for her willingness to share her husband, Mark, with his high school friends, even when he had so little time left on this earth, and for reminding me that "through sickness and in health" is more than just ceremonial gibberish. To Hunter and Lauren Feeley, your father was a great man who always encouraged me to write, and he is sorely missed.

In addition to many of those listed above, I'd also like to thank the following people for helping me by reading and offering their critique of these stories: Eavan Alvarez, Paul Hirchak, Jeanette Hirchak, Lauren Hirchak and Joseph Hirchak. I am also grateful to the following artists, who helped fill in gaps by providing illustrations where none existed before: Margot Beberaggi and Jennifer Robbins.

I also need to recognize the members of the Hoggard High School boys' tennis team for the inspiration they provided to me during my final four grueling months of writing. Instead of accepting the preconceived opinions of their naysayers and doubters, they believed in themselves and supported one another throughout their journey to both conference champions and to the round-of-eight in the North Carolina State Championship. Not only did they help free my mind from the obsession of this book, but they also helped me better understand the indomitable will of the heroic characters that appear in these stories. Congratulations and thank you to: Coach Michael Bowen, Coach Tim Hower, Noah Milliken, Chase Horton, Evan Linett, Matt Jensen, Miles Hirchak, Dom Scialabba, Dillon Cook, Andrew Haskins, Yue Zhang and Cadman Styers.

I want to extend a very special thank-you to Mike Hartle, for taking the time to proofread these stories to ensure they are written properly and to help remind me that I am no e.e. cummings. You, sir, are responsible for all grammatical errors in this book! Of course, you, the reader, should also be grateful of Mike's mastery of the English language. But of coarse without, he - *gift* of grammar, (however) but most "certainly' definitely, this; boook wood reed. Like! This: no lie?

I also need to thank my wonderful stepdaughter, Kellie Miller Hall, for being there when we needed each other the most and for bringing Jesse, Tyler and Katelyn with you. Your helping Kim and Miles during my writing process means the world to me, and I appreciate your willingness to sit down and listen to the stories be read out loud. I also love having the four of you in my family.

To my mother, Anne Hirchak, thank you for instilling in me the courage to persist against overwhelming odds. Just after I started writing this book, she was diagnosed with cancer for the third time in her life. After an invasive surgery, weakened to the point of exhaustion and wanting nothing more than to get back to her volunteer work with children, she faithfully took the time to read every single story included in this book. Though she is a voracious reader, she wants you to know these are some of the best stories ever written. I love you, Mom! I also want to thank my mom's good friends Cheryl Johnson, Barbara Wilson and Dee Davis for helping my mom during her recovery and giving me the extra time I needed to work on these stories.

To my son, Miles, I owe a very special super-ultimate, roaring "THANK YOU" for affording me the time to write late into the evening, for allowing me to miss a few of his tennis tournaments and music recitals and for never complaining when he asked me to throw a Frisbee, hit tennis balls or go for a bike ride and I had to reply, "I can't because I have to write." (Though he quickly learned when he said, "Dad, let's go get an ice cream," it always worked!) You are my beautiful boy…er, young man, and every day, you make me proud to be your father. I have never met anyone with a sweeter, kinder soul than yours. My love for you is endless.

Finally, to my beautiful wife, Kim. No one encouraged me more, or sacrificed as much, as you. In addition to your already full plate, you willingly took on my entire workload. During my absence, you ran our businesses, family and household and never once complained. (OK, there was that one time, but it really was my fault.) Despite all the obstacles thrown in my way, you urged me on. In fairness, this book is really yours. You earned it! I often think my life has been a series of accidents culminating in the now, yet I don't believe our meeting was an accident. I believe it was destiny. You are, and will forever remain, my one and only true love.

# INTRODUCTION

This book was almost never written. I know this sounds trite, like some cheap literary cliché, but it's the truth. It has taken eight months, three extensions and countless hours staring at a jumble of words on a computer screen. Several times, I was prepared to call it quits. But each time that I struggled with doubt, exhaustion and what felt like endless frustration, I tried to stay focused on one underlying fact: this book had to be written. Not for you, the reader, and not for the amazing lives that fill these pages, but for me, the author. In many ways, this book is my salvation.

When I published *Ghosts of Old Wilmington* in 2006, I immediately wanted to write another book. But I had a new tour to research, develop and write: the Hollywood Location Walk. In 2007, I found I had a pile of incomplete stories to tackle and add to our existing tours: the Ghost Walk of Old Wilmington and the Haunted Pub Crawl. Then in 2008, my wife decided she wanted to open a store, the Black Cat Shoppe, in downtown Wilmington. Finally, in 2009, I felt like I was ready. I began assembling ideas and making notes. Then, on March 4, 2009, Lindsay Marie Miller, my wife's daughter, my son's sister and my step-daughter, passed away. She was only eighteen. She was full of so much promise and had her whole life ahead of her. She had been part of my existence for sixteen years, and then suddenly and unexpectedly, she was gone. I have lost many people in my life, but absolutely nothing compares to this. On March 4, 2009, a piece of my soul was extinguished.

I found I no longer had the passion to write. I tried. In 2011, I made several discreet attempts, working late at night, without my wife's or son's knowledge, in hope that somehow the written word would break through, that the magic of creation would rekindle my love of the art. But each time it ended in failure, with my head buried in my hands, weeping. I found it impossible to create life within a story when inside a part of me felt like it was dying. As the years passed, I found the process too painful, and I thought it was best to just give up writing. And so I did.

Tragically, it was another death that roused me from my self-induced muteness. On March 5, 2013, Mark Thomas Aquinas Feeley, one of my oldest and dearest friends, succumbed to pancreatic cancer, after a two-year battle. The next morning, I got in my car and drove to New York. During the drive, I reflected on how unrelenting time is. There is no make-up and no redo. Life simply is. This was to be the first spark.

When I returned home to my family, I gave serious thought to my four years of silence. I knew if there was any hope of my finding my voice, I had to begin writing something, anything. After several failed attempts, I finally wrote one new Haunted Pub Crawl story, one that had been sitting on my desk for over four years. The result was awful. But I kept rewriting it until I got it right. I finally wrote something new! Then one day, while at lunch with my wife, I blurted out, "I want to write another book." The statement lingered in the air like some unfamiliar odor. It took my wife several seconds to realize what I had just said. Then, as she has always done for me, she said, "Of course you do, and you will," as though it was so obvious all along. That night, I told my son, and true to form, his teenage indifference spoke volumes. I thought, "I am ready!"

When I first proposed this book to The History Press, I had no real idea what I wanted to write. I had a collection of old stories from old tours that I thought would work, but nothing concrete. The publisher accepted my proposal, thanks in no small part to the relationship we already had from my first book. However, almost immediately after signing the contract, my mother was diagnosed with cancer. Then my wife was offered an opportunity to open a second store, Jokilimi Island Imports. Suddenly, I felt overwhelmed. I called my editor, and he kindly offered me an extension.

I decided the best thing to do was to tackle the longest, most difficult story that I knew I wanted to include in this book and then take it from there. What an idiot. It's like deciding to climb Everest after breaking both legs rather than learning how to walk with crutches. But between my mom's surgery and recovery and my wife's preparation for the new store, I slogged through the first story. During the long ordeal, I began perusing and dropping stories from my list of possibilities. I finally settled on the ones included here. I didn't realize it until much later, while trying to work with The History Press at formulating a title, but the stories all had a common thread: the lives covered were all legendary.

I will be honest: I shed a lot of tears while writing these stories, even the funny ones. It has been an incredibly emotional and arduous journey of self-discovery. In the end, I learned something new about myself, and I have intentionally saved this thought to make sure it is the last sentence I type in the completion of my book. I will never be the same person I was when I fell asleep on the night of March 3, 2009, but today, at the very least, I can once again happily say, I am a writer.

# 1

# THE YEAST THAT BINDS

My father met Pee Wee in 1950 in basic training. The two men, along with tens of thousands of others, were preparing for what looked like inevitable war in Korea. By the time my father and Pee Wee were deployed, they were fast friends. They, like many young men who prepare for battle, had come to terms with their own mortality. The two friends agreed that if, for any reason, one of them failed to make it through the war, the survivor would forever offer the first sip of a newly popped beer to the memory of the one who had fallen. Pee Wee did not survive the war. So no matter where my father was or what the occasion, whenever he opened a beer, he would bow his head; whisper, "To Pee Wee"; and then spill the first sip to the ground. As a little boy, watching my father ritually pay homage to a fallen comrade, I began to understand the intrinsic spiritual and patriotic value of beer as it related to the American experience.

## An American Tradition

The history of beer in America began in 1587, when colonists brewed their first ale with corn. In 1607, the first imported beer reached the New World, but for the most part, the colonists could not afford such costly goods. So in 1609, the colonies began recruiting English brewers to join them in America. Yet in 1620, when the *Mayflower* arrived at Plymouth Rock, beer was still in short supply. The crew, fearing they might not have enough beer for their return voyage, quickly ushered the Pilgrims ashore and set sail. Eventually, trade with mother England reached the point where most colonists, especially along the coast, were able to afford the finer British beers, and imports steadily rose. By the mid-1700s, porter, a mix of light and dark malts, was created and quickly became a favorite with dockhands, soldiers and the working class. By 1770, the average colonist consumed thirty-four gallons of beer, five gallons of distilled spirits (mainly rum) and one gallon of wine annually.

Porter, like all other beers, is dependent on yeast to carry out fermentation. Yeast essentially converts carbohydrates into alcohol and carbon dioxide. Before yeast is added during the final stages of brewing, the liquid concoction is called "hopped wort." It's only after the yeast is added and the fermentation is complete that it officially becomes "beer." For many eighteenth-century brewers, their yeast strain was their most protected secret ingredient.

## The Rouse's Tavern Massacre

Taverns, often referred to as public houses or "pubs," played an important role in colonial America. The tavern was a gathering place and a link to the overall world. It was a place to socialize, share news of the day, administer law and conduct business. It was also an ideal environment to discuss insurrection. In fact, much of the planning and organizing for the American Revolution took place in taverns.

Rouse's Tavern was located eight miles north of Wilmington on the Old New Bern Road (present-day Market Street, near Ogden). Before and during the war, the tavern was a gathering place for many revolutionaries such as Cornelius Harnett, known as the Samuel Adams of North Carolina and the colony's most influential revolutionary; William Hooper, a signer of the Declaration of Independence; Major General Robert Howe, who later was in command of the Continental army's Southern Department; Lieutenant Colonel Thomas Bludworth, a former tavern owner and gunsmith who proved merciless against Wilmington's Loyalist and Tory factions; and Major James Love, who, like his good friend Bludworth, was ruthless in his treatment of Loyalists, Tories and, later, British troops.

After the British occupied Wilmington on January 29, 1781, Bludworth and Love led a campaign of harassment against the occupiers. A popular tactic was to kill the British sentries along the roads leading into Wilmington

Pubs like Rouse's Tavern (also known as the Eight Mile House because of its distance from Wilmington), were an important gathering place for revolutionaries before and during the War for Independence. *Illustration by John Hirchak.*

and then hide out and ambush the dragoons that were sent to capture them. By February, Major James Craig, who was in charge of the occupation, had issued orders for the capture or killing of both Bludworth and Love.

In March, Major Love and about a dozen Patriots, under orders from Brigadier General Alexander Lillington, were busy rustling cattle in the vicinity of present-day Military Cutoff Road in order to keep them out of British hands. After one typical foray, Love and his men stopped by Rouse's Tavern for a taste of brew. Despite an act of war, no man was beyond partaking in a pint of fine English porter. As the men drank, laughed and regaled one another with recent wartime escapades, evening enveloped them. It was just after midnight when the men decided that, rather than return to camp, they would sleep on the tavern floor and ride out at first light. Feeling secure in their surroundings, a sentry was not posted.

Unbeknownst to Major Love, Major Craig had been made aware of the militiamen's presence at Rouse's Tavern. Craig led at least sixty redcoats on a quick march to the pub. Upon their arrival, Craig issued an order that no quarter be given. The redcoats quietly entered the tavern and bayonetted and shot to death at least ten men, many of whom were still asleep. Major Love was awakened and attempted to escape, slashing wildly with his cutlass and using his saddle as a shield. He made it out the front door, but the redcoats quickly surrounded him, forcing him to retreat to a mulberry tree about thirty yards from the tavern. The redcoats attacked en masse, goring Love to death with their bayonets.

When Bludworth, who was camped perhaps a mile away, heard shots being fired, he gathered his militia and rode in the direction of Rouse's Tavern. By the time the Patriots arrived, the British were long gone. Bludworth and his men immediately came upon the gored remains of Major Love. The militiamen entered the tavern and discovered the bloody carnage. An old woman and several children who were witness to the massacre were found huddled near the fireplace. The old woman told Bludworth how the redcoats had murdered the men in their sleep. She also said one Patriot was taken alive and questioned about the whereabouts of other militiamen, assured that he would be released unharmed if he cooperated. The Patriot told the redcoats that three militiamen could be found at a farm a few miles up the road. The redcoats then shot the Patriot through the head. Bludworth was incensed and swore revenge for those who died in what was to become known as the Rouse's Tavern Massacre.

## OLD BESS

Over the next few months, Bludworth designed and built an especially long-barreled rifle capable of accurately carrying a special two-ounce ball up to seven hundred yards distance. He named the rifle "Old Bess" and practiced until he was proficient. On July 4, Bludworth; his eldest son, Tim; and Jim Paget, a family friend, paddled a canoe with a week's worth of rations out to Point Peter, just north of the city where the two branches of the Cape Fear River converged. Upon their arrival, Bludworth shared his plan to snipe British soldiers in revenge for the Rouse's Tavern Massacre. He told

British redcoats along Hanover Street, directly across the river from Point Peter. From *The British in Wilmington,* Howard Pyle (1853–1911). *Courtesy of Library of Congress.*

Tim and Paget that if either man wished to leave, they could do so without reprisal. They all agreed to remain together.

At the time, Point Peter was studded with old-growth cypress trees. The monarch (or largest) tree was a seven-foot-diameter behemoth that rose at least seventy feet in height before coming to the first of its branches. From all outward appearances, this cypress was solid; however, the lower portion was actually hollow. The hollow could be accessed only from a well-concealed tunnel a few feet from the base. Once inside the tree, the men built a platform and used an auger to drill several holes through the trunk, both for light and for a clear view of the Wilmington docks that ran along the eastern shore of the Cape Fear River. Bludworth was confident that the prevalent downriver winds would help mask the smoke from each shot and conceal their whereabouts.

Twice a day, British troops gathered along the docks between Princess and Grace Streets in order to receive their rum rations. The British had long issued daily alcohol rations to their troops. Up until 1655, British sailors were issued a daily ration of one gallon of beer. After 1655, when Jamaica was brought under British rule, some naval captains began issuing rum. By 1740, the Royal Navy officially issued half a pint of strong rum daily—half at noon and half at sunset. By 1756, the British military had switched to grog (two parts water to one part rum) and, shortly thereafter, began adding lime or lemon juice to combat scurvy (thus the nickname "limey").

Though the rum ration ceremony implies that only rum or grog were served, the army often substituted other alcoholic beverages, including French brandy, strong wine, claret, spruce beer or porter. In 1775 alone, British troops received 375,000 gallons of porter for their daily rations. Whatever the drink, the men would be called to gather and the ration distributed. Typically an ornate, brass-lined barrel or rum tub was used to serve the drink. After the men received their rations, toasts would be raised, and then the men would consume their liquor.

As the redcoats and dragoons gathered in the vicinity of Nelson's Pub, Bludworth took aim and fired. The redcoats were taken by surprise when a fellow soldier's head snapped back from a bloody head shot. Four soldiers quickly grabbed the downed man and dragged him into Nelson's. The remaining soldiers scanned the surrounding area, unsure from which direction the shot had come. Moments later, a second soldier's head snapped back, and he, too, fell. As he was dragged into Nelson's, the remaining redcoats and dragoons quickly began searching the shoreline, but a third shot sent them scurrying.

For days, Bludworth and his accomplices used Old Bess to great effect, shooting and killing British soldiers up and down the Wilmington riverfront. Though the British searched the eastern shore of the river and along Eagles Island, they never crossed over to Point Peter, believing it was simply too great a distance for anyone to snipe from. It wasn't until a week of terror had passed and dozens of redcoats and dragoons had fallen that a Loyalist arrived in town and mentioned seeing three men with an extremely long rifle canoeing out to Point Peter. That afternoon, twenty redcoats were dispatched with orders to cut down every tree on the point. As one tree after another fell, Bludworth and his accomplices remained hidden in their hollow. At nightfall, the troops bedded down, and the three men crawled out of the tunnel and made their way to their hidden canoe. A sleeping British sentinel awoke to the sounds of rustling reeds and called out, "Who goes there?" Bludworth imitated the snort of a wild pig, and the sentinel was fooled into believing it was nothing more than an animal. The guard eventually fell back to sleep, and the three men escaped.

# THE BOTTLE WRECK

On the eastern shore of the River Arun in West Sussex, England, sits the village of Littlehampton. In 1825, an English brig carrying casks and

The Original Flag Porter 1825. The ship on the label is a depiction of the English brig that sank off Littlehampton, today known as the Bottle Wreck. *Courtesy of Darwin Brewery.*

bottles of a special porter bound for America was lost in the rough seas of the English Channel just offshore of Littlehampton. The loss of a single ship was of little notice since over one thousand British ships sank in 1825 alone. It wasn't until 163 years later that the ship, or at least its cargo, became significant.

In 1988, Dr. Keith Thomas, a prominent microbiologist who worked for an English brewing, analysis and training company named Brewlab, was attending a workshop on the history and brewing techniques for classic English porter. Dr. Thomas was interested in re-creating a porter based on an original, early nineteenth-century recipe and was looking for ideas on how to reclaim the integrity of this particular beer. While at the workshop, Dr. Thomas overheard a conversation about an English brig that went down off the coast of Littlehampton in 1825. In 1983, divers discovered the wreck and recovered a significant number of half-pint porter bottles. Though the wreck is officially listed as Site 5013, due to the number of bottles scattered throughout the debris field, divers affectionately refer to the site as the "Bottle Wreck."

Shortly after the workshop, Brewlab sponsored a dive on the Bottle Wreck in hopes of finding something that would help them re-create their nineteenth-century porter. To Dr. Thomas's delight, the dive team successfully recovered two unbroken half-pint bottles with intact corks and wax seals. Intact seals meant the contents were uncompromised, and there was a chance the original strain of yeast used to brew the porter might have survived.

Under normal conditions, it would be highly unlikely for a yeast fungus to survive for 163 years. Light, air and heat would eventually break down the yeast. However, because the Bottle Wreck rested in sixty feet of dark, frigid English Channel water and the bottles were sealed closed, it was possible for a few cells of yeast to survive. There was concern the first bottle had become contaminated, so tests were carefully conducted on the contents of the second bottle. Culturing initially resulted in nothing but bacteria and mold growth, but then, after numerous failed attempts, a single strain of yeast was produced. By using the original recipe, early nineteenth-century brewing techniques and this original strain of yeast, Dr. Thomas was able to create (not re-create), an original porter. Darwin Brewery, UK, bought the rights to the recipe and began brewing and aging the beer as the Original Flag Porter 1825. In 1991, the beer was reintroduced to the world.

# Walt

After British troops withdrew from Wilmington on November 18, 1781, the riverfront developed around the shipping industry's needs: docks, warehouses and offices. After the state docks opened a few miles farther downriver in 1952 and the departure of the railroad in 1960, Wilmington fell into a period of indifference. One by one, the old shipping and railroad structures were torn down. The riverfront, for the most part, grew stagnant from disinterest and disuse. Then, in the early 1990s, Wilmington began to experience a renaissance. A strong downtown revitalization effort, as well as a keen interest in saving the city's past, brought new life to the riverfront.

In 1999, half of a hideous riverfront parking deck—built in 1966 atop the stretch of land near where Nelson's Pub once sat and where dozens of British soldiers fell to Thomas Bludworth's long rifle—was torn down. The following year, a nine-story condominium complex was built, with the upper eight floors reserved for residential use and the ground floor for retail. It was in one of these units that Cape Fear Wine & Beer opened in 2003. The pub's goal was to introduce locals to hundreds of rare, interesting, classic and exotic beers from around the country and the world. And so it was fitting that shortly after opening, a brewery rep, whose portfolio happened to include hard-to-find English beers, dropped in.

As the staff gathered, the rep went into his sales pitch. He started to rattle off a few of the more common English beers and why he thought they might be a good fit for the pub. But it was soon evident that the folks at Cape Fear Wine & Beer weren't interested in a sales pitch. So the rep stopped talking, reached into his bag and withdrew a bottle of Original Flag Porter 1825. He placed it on the bar, and the demeanor of the group suddenly changed.

The rep told them the story of how the porter came to be. He showed off the bottle's label, which depicted a drawing of the English brig that became known as the Bottle Wreck after it sank all those years ago. He then popped the bottle and almost reverently poured a few ounces into several glasses, commenting on the dark mahogany color and frothy head. "This," he said, "is the closest you will come to a traditional porter." And though the staff heartily agreed that the porter would be a welcome addition to their pub, what proved to be most memorable about that day was something the rep said just before he downed his portion of the porter. One of his ancestors (whom he called Walt), served under Major James Craig, and, he said, it is quite possible that Walt drank this exact same porter while here in Wilmington. Perhaps, he added, even while sitting at or near this very spot, for this is just how original this recipe is.

When the first shipment of the Original Flag Porter 1825 arrived at Cape Fear Wine & Beer, it was assigned a narrow berth in one of the wall-to-wall coolers that ran the entire length of the south side of the pub. The

The alcove to Cape Fear Wine & Beer. Beyond these doors, the ghost of Walt can still be found, seeking out his daily ration of porter. *Photo by John Hirchak.*

beer was one of over three hundred available, and with so many siblings, it would need to prove it was special in order to stand out from the crowd. And indeed, this is exactly what happened.

The first occurrence took place just after closing time on the first night the new porter had arrived. The staff had locked up and was busy mopping and cleaning when, suddenly, the door began violently jerking back and forth, as though someone were frantically trying to get in. There was no one standing outside the front door while it rattled back and forth. A few nights later, it happened again. A few nights later still, a staff member, who was the last to leave, was standing out front of the pub, locking the front door. When he glanced up, he saw a shadowy figure pacing in front of the cooler doors, along the section where the Original Flag Porter 1825 was perched. The shadow was not well defined, and there were no discernable features, but it clearly appeared to be moving back and forth in front of this section of cooler. This, too, soon became a common occurrence. It also became common for this particular cooler door to open and close of its own accord. The staff soon became convinced that this apparition was none other than the ghost of a fallen redcoat in need of a fresh bottle of porter. They began referring to the ghost as Walt.

But the most memorable of all of Walt's shenanigans was yet to come. Months passed, and the staff and patrons reveled in Walt's typical escapades.

Then one afternoon, between the midday crowd and the evening crowd, Walt cemented his legend. That afternoon's bartender had just finished leveling the cooler shelves (turning all the labels outward and pulling the bottles forward toward the cooler doors). Upon finishing the section of cooler that held the porters, he closed the door and reached for the handle on the adjacent cooler. Suddenly, from inside the cooler, came an explosive "pop." He jumped back, imagining that one of the florescent tubes that helped light each cooler had fallen loose and burst on the concrete floor. However, it was soon obvious there were no cooler lights out. After a few minutes of searching, he came upon the row of Original Flag Porter 1825. The head of the front bottle was snapped at the neck, and after a quick search, he found it lying on the floor of the cooler, the cap still intact. This alone would have been unsettling, for the head was cleanly broken off. But what was most startling was that all the porter that should have been either inside the bottle or splashed somewhere around the cooler, was missing. Not a drop was left to be found. The porter simply vanished.

A few years ago, Cape Fear Wine & Beer moved exactly one block up, off the river, almost directly behind its original location. In the process of moving, there was concern that Walt would remain behind in the old pub. Some of the staff members, and quite a few patrons, urged Walt to join them at the new location. The question remained, where was Walt's loyalty? But to the pub's delight, shortly after relocating, the staff found another shattered head of Original Flag Porter 1825! Since the move, Cape Fear Wine & Beer has introduced several other original porters made from this same strain of yeast. And to the staff's and patrons' amazement, some of these new porters, like the Original Flag Porter 1825—and like the redcoats of 1781—suffer the same head wounds.

# CAUSAL LINKS

Shortly after this story was added to the Haunted Pub Crawl, a guest of the tour expressed doubt about how a single cell of one strain of yeast could link four separate events on two different continents over the course of 230 years. Isn't it just as likely, she asked, that there is no causal link between any of these people or any of these events? And I will admit, for a short period of time, she created doubt in my mind. Then one night, I witnessed a bartender handing a young marine a beer. Initially, I wasn't sure why I found this intriguing, but something kept me looking. Then, suddenly, the marine bowed his head, whispered something inaudible and spilled a little sip of beer on the bar. And at that moment the universe collapsed to just the three of us, sharing in the ritual of paying homage to a fallen comrade, just as I had watched my father do a thousand times before. The marine looked back up at the bartender, and the two men, lips pursed, eyes full of anguish, respectfully nodded to each other, and I, too, nodded with them. And I finally realized that this is exactly how a single cell of one strain of yeast can connect us all.

# 2

# TOPSY

The Hagenbeck-Wallace Circus was accustomed to tragedy. In 1913, eight elephants, eight horses and over twenty lions and tigers drowned in the Wabash River flood. Five years later, on June 22, 1918, a train engineer who had fallen asleep at his controls plowed his locomotive into the rear of a fully loaded, twenty-six-car Hagenbeck-Wallace circus train. The old wooden boxcars and passenger cars shattered into piles of debris, which abruptly caught fire from the old oil lamps used for lighting. Between the transient nature of the circus and the fact that the bodies were burned beyond recognition, it is estimated that of the 400 showmen aboard the circus train, between 86 and 104 died and 127 were injured, making it the worst train disaster in American history.

If not for the training techniques developed by Carl Hagenbeck, this story might also have ended in tragedy. Hagenbeck, an animal trainer, had long been appalled by the fear-based methods used to train and control circus animals. In response, he pioneered a gentler, and much more productive, reward-based program. These methods not only produced better-trained, calmer animals, but they also helped create a more thorough, nurturing bond between trainer and animal. Though Hagenbeck later sold his interest in the circus, his reward-based techniques took hold, and today, they are the basis for circus animal training worldwide.

In October 1922, the Hagenbeck-Wallace Circus—at the time, part of the second largest circus in America—came to Wilmington. After its tents were set up in an open field at South Thirteenth and Ann Streets, the circus generated a lot of local excitement by staging a carnival-like parade through downtown Wilmington. Despite an incessant, lingering rain, the circus conducted two sold-out performances. At the conclusion of the final evening's show, the roustabouts, with the assistance of the elephants, began breaking down the cumbersome tents. Under the cover of darkness, heavy rain and booming thunderclaps, nobody noticed Topsy, a four-ton Indian elephant (a subspecies of the Asian elephant), slip away.

Despite her weight, Topsy was a fleet-footed pachyderm. She quickly made her way to Brooklyn, one and a half miles northwest of the circus grounds. At the time, the circus was still unaware of Topsy's disappearance, and the police were unaware they had a runaway elephant in their midst. So when the first call came in to the police station from a frantic resident on Swann Street, the police assumed the caller was drunk.

"You won't believe this," the caller stated, "but there's a varmint in my vegetable garden pulling up my collards with his tail and stuffing them up his rear end, and I hope you can come get it."

Of course, Topsy was not ripping the man's collards out of the ground with her tail and stuffing them in her rear end; she was using her trunk and feeding them into her mouth. It's easy to understand the man's mistake, considering it was nighttime, he was looking through a rain-smudged window and he had never seen an elephant before. Despite their skepticism, the police dispatched a car, and though the garden's fencing was trampled and the collards were torn out of the ground and missing, this mysterious butt-stuffing creature was nowhere to be found.

Then a second call came into the station, this time from nearly two miles southeast of Brooklyn, just five blocks east of the circus grounds. The caller, who lived on Carolina Avenue, had been to the circus performance earlier that evening. She calmly explained to the police that there was an elephant in her backyard and she needed a policeman to come remove it. While en route, the police were notified by the circus that they did indeed have a stray pachyderm on their hands; however, by the time they arrived, Topsy was long gone.

Suddenly, the police were being inundated with calls from frantic residents. A woman in the 600 block of Walnut Street reported seeing a large gray mule running down her alleyway. One of her neighbors heard a deafening series of crashes and found several large sections of his fencing torn down. Another neighbor awoke to a tremendous boom and a shaking house, as Topsy inadvertently bumped into the man's home, knocking over a pillar on his front porch. The half-naked homeowner jumped from his bed and raced into the street, shouting, "Earthquake! Earthquake!" It took a considerable amount of time for police officers to calm the man and convince him that his house had actually been hit by an elephant, not an earthquake.

A few blocks west, in an alleyway near Third and Market Streets, Topsy was seen and heard crashing through a series of backyard fences, flattening everything in her path. A man claimed he saw Topsy charging across his backyard, wearing a chicken coop around her neck. This led to a local newspaper erroneously claiming that during her rampage Topsy had actually eaten well over one hundred chickens! Of course, elephants are herbivores. She didn't eat them, she stepped on them.

As the police frantically searched for the missing elephant, Topsy made her way to the Eureka Pressing Company, a tanning and dye business, on the corner of Dock and South Second Streets. The Eureka Pressing Company had large plate glass windows on the front of its store, and as Topsy ambled by, she apparently saw her reflection. Elephants, being social creatures, stopped to say hello. As she excitedly approached her fellow pachyderm, she was surprised to suddenly find herself crashing through a window and standing inside of a building. Worse still, there was no fellow elephant to greet her. Angry at not finding a companion, Topsy rumbled through the building, trampling everything in her path. Thirsty from her labor, she mistakenly sucked up a trunk full of clothes dye from a large wooden vat. At first taste, she found the liquid repulsive and spat the dye across the room, ruining hundreds of garments.

Daylight was approaching, and Topsy, ready for greener pastures, leaned her enormous bulk against the south side of the store, collapsing the brick wall. She then continued on her journey two miles south, disappearing into the swamps between Greenfield Lake and the Cape Fear River. She must have believed she had made it back to her Indian homeland, for she sunk to her belly in the bog, eating, drinking, sleeping and resting.

The city awoke to the startling news that a chicken-eating, earthquake-inducing elephant with a rectum full of collards was on the loose. Residents were enthralled. Papers up and down the East Coast carried the story. When she was discovered hiding out in the swamps near Greenfield Lake, hundreds of Wilmingtonians flocked to the area in hopes of catching a glimpse of this amazing beast.

In an effort to escape her throng of rabid fans, Topsy pressed deeper into the swamp. She soon found herself buried chest-deep in muck and unable to move. As the police kept the crowds at bay, a single officer, Leon George, entered the quagmire and approached the helpless elephant. Officer George realized Topsy's predicament and decided he had to do something to help this poor creature. So he carefully approached Topsy and knelt beside her.

The former Eureka Pressing Company. Large, plate glass windows once lined the left side and front of the building. The wall on the right was collapsed during Topsy's escape. The building is currently part of the Wilmingtonian Inn. *Photo by Kim Hirchak.*

"Come on, Mumsey, you can do this," he encouraged her. "Come on little girl. You've got this. Come on sweetheart."

Throughout the day, Officer George urged the elephant on. Using her mighty trunk, Topsy would grab the base of a tree and pull herself forward. Inch by inch, she slowly advanced. Hour after hour, Officer George beckoned her on. Whole trees were toppled from her effort. But as night fell, there was a near-consensus that Topsy was growing fatigued and would be unable to free herself. The mighty elephant was spent and would most certainly die. But having looked into the eyes of this beautiful, intelligent mammal, Officer George refused to quit. He remained by her side in the now-chilly swampland, urging her on: "Come on Mumsey, you've got to pull harder. I won't let you quit, little girl. Come on Mumsey, you've got to do this!"

As night tightened its grip and the temperature dropped, the crowd gathered outside the swamp along the roadway grew subdued. There were whispers of Topsy's ultimate demise. But Officer George, whom local newspapers now referred to as the "Tiger Hunter," continued to press Topsy, tempting her with peanuts, apples and other elephant treats. Finally, with a great sucking sound, Topsy pulled herself free from the swamp. Trumpeting loudly, she approached Officer George and gently caressed his head with her trunk, a sign of affection. Then, purring in a way similar to a cat, Topsy allowed Officer George to lead her out by the trunk. As Officer George and an exhausted Topsy emerged from the dark forest, hundreds of Wilmingtonians broke out in cheer.

The sluggish elephant was led along Front Street, back into the heart of downtown Wilmington. With each passing block, the crowd grew in size, chanting and cheering for Topsy. As she made her way to the old train depot on North Front Street, the reception seemed to lift her spirits. Then, as she was mere steps from the ramp leading up to the old bull-car that was preparing to whisk her away, she decided it was time for an encore. With an abrupt change in direction, she trotted off toward the river, the crowd chanting, "Topsy! Topsy! Topsy!"

Without so much as a pause, Topsy ran off the end of the dock and plunged into the river with a tremendous splash. Then, paddling with all her might, she disappeared into the night, headed in the general direction of Point Peter.

It wasn't until the following afternoon that Topsy, with the aid of Officer George, was recaptured. But before a barge could arrive to help carry her back to the eastern shore of Cape Fear, she again broke free. Throughout the day and into the night, she eluded capture in the swampy south end between Point Peter and Muddy Point. Finally, the next morning, Officer George, again with a handful of apples, peanuts and other elephant treats, lured Topsy across the river to Eagles Island. After a brief reunion with her new best friend, her legs were secured with chains.

When Topsy was again paraded through town, there were thousands of people cheering her on. Though she had traversed fifteen miles throughout the city and caused tens of thousands of dollars in damage, aside from a few flattened chickens, she had caused no physical harm. As Topsy ascended the ramp into her private bull-car, she paused and the entire crowd gasped, wondering if she was about to embark on yet another encore. Then, Topsy turned her head as though to acknowledge her legion of fans. Her gaze fell upon Officer Leon "Tiger Hunter" George, who was openly weeping. And

This 1922 photograph, thought to be one of the few surviving images of Topsy the elephant, shows her being led down a bull-car ramp of the Hagenbeck-Wallace Circus. *Courtesy of Circus World Museum, Baraboo, Wisconsin.*

then, with what many swore was a look of triumph, Topsy slightly bowed her head before stepping into the bull-car. The crowd promptly erupted into frantic applause.

That is how Topsy the elephant became a legend in Wilmington, North Carolina.

3

# MAGGIE HOLLADAY

In 1889, William and Maggie Holladay began construction on their new American Queen Anne–style home in downtown Wilmington. Not only were they building their first home together, but also Maggie was pregnant with their second child. It was hoped the home would be completed in time for the family to move in and for Maggie to give birth there. What a wonderful way to christen your first home together: with the birth of a child.

As the home was nearing completion and furnishings were being delivered, the first hints of labor appeared. Maggie tried to soothe Nannie, her very worried five-year-old daughter. Don't cry, be strong and everything will be fine, she told her. The family doctor was summoned, and Nannie was escorted from the room.

Maggie's birthing cries were soon chorused by the joyful wail of a healthy baby girl, Marguerite. But Maggie's cries didn't end. There was an inordinate amount of blood. The newborn was quickly ushered from the room as the doctor attempted to stop Maggie's hemorrhaging, but the blood flow wouldn't abate. Marguerite was returned to the room and briefly placed in her mother's arms moments before twenty-four-year-old Maggie passed away.

Though William was devastated, Nannie was nearly inconsolable. She believed her mother died because Nannie didn't stop crying and worrying like her mother asked. The following day, at Maggie's wake, Nannie broke free of her father's hand and raced across the room. She flung herself across her mother's body and began shaking her, screaming, "Please wake up, Mommy. I promise I'll be good!" Poor William had to carry a wailing

Maggie and William Holladay's beautiful American Queen Anne–style home was completed in 1889, just prior to Maggie's death while giving birth to her daughter Marguerite. *Photo courtesy of the Reichert family.*

Nannie from the room and again explain to her that Mommy was gone and could not come back.

Almost immediately, William began to experience the presence of Maggie in the new house. On more than one occasion, Marguerite would be upstairs napping while William sat in the downstairs parlor reading. When the baby would awaken, she would begin crying. If William didn't immediately put his book down and go up to her (perhaps he wanted to finish a paragraph first), when he finally did begin to ascend the stairs, he would hear footsteps race past him and feel a petticoat brushing against his legs.

Late one evening, William awoke to the sounds of Nannie giggling. He put on his robe and walked down the dark hallway. As he approached the middle bedroom, he heard Nannie laugh. When William stepped into the doorway, he found Nannie sitting on the floor with her back to him. Several of her dolls were spread out before her. Nannie pointed to one of the dolls, whispered something and then began giggling uncontrollably. William stepped into the otherwise empty room and placed his hand on Nannie's shoulder.

"Nannie, are you OK?"

Nannie, trying to suppress her laugh, looked up at her father.

"It's OK, Daddy. Mommy and I are just playing."

It was then that William accepted that Maggie had never really left the children. In fact, every family who has ever lived in the Holladay house has had their own encounter with Maggie's ghost. One woman tells a story of a bridge club that would meet at the house every Wednesday. While playing cards, they would occasionally hear the footsteps of Maggie walking around each table, as though inspecting each hand. And then, as though a card had been misplayed, one would be brushed off the table and flutter down to the floor.

Another family came downstairs one Christmas morning and found Maggie's apparition standing in front of their tree, inspecting the ornaments. The gauzy figure would take an ornament in her hand and pull it toward her, causing the branch of the tree to bend slightly. After a few moments' inspection, she would let go and it would bounce back into place. They said this went on for about a minute before the figure slowly faded away and was gone.

Sometimes, Maggie would be seen at the top of the staircase on the second floor. She always wore the same black hoop dress and was only seen from behind. Other times, she was seen walking down the hallway and into the master bedroom. But more often than not, her presence was felt in the middle bedroom. In this bedroom, parents would occasionally find their own children's toys stacked in the middle of the room, as though Maggie were waiting for Nannie or Marguerite's return so she could have some afternoon play.

The carved bust that, when held, whispered, "I am Maggie" to an owner of the Holladay home. *Photo courtesy of the Reichert family.*

One owner had an interesting encounter with Maggie outside of the home. The woman said she was intrigued by Maggie's story but indifferent about ghosts. That same day she found herself in an antique store on Front Street, going through some recently acquired bins from a downtown estate sale. She came across an old mahogany bust of a woman. She lifted the heavy piece out of the crate and looked into the eyes of the carving. She thought to herself, "This is the most beautiful face I have ever seen." As she completed this thought, another voice, not her own, entered her mind and whispered, "I am Maggie." The woman nearly dropped the piece and fled. But she didn't. Rather, she purchased the bust and placed it on the mantle in the main parlor. For her, this was indeed the bust of Maggie Holladay.

In July 2002, while conducting a Ghost Walk of Old Wilmington tour, I decided to stop by the Holladay house and share Maggie's story. It had been at least six months since I was last by the Holladay house, but there were so many families on the tour that night (and parents really connect well with this story) that at the last minute, I decided to add it to my route. As the group gathered beneath the sprawling live oak out front of the home, I started: "In 1889, William and Maggie Holladay…"

From the back of the group, a man and a woman gasped loudly. The woman covered her mouth with her hand while the man's eyes began welling up. I thought, "Wow, I am so *on* tonight!" But as I continued on with the story, I couldn't help but notice how the couple's anguish grew. When I got to the part where Nannie broke free of her father's grasp and flung herself across her mother's body, the couple sobbed. By the time I got to Nannie turning to her father and saying, "It's OK, Daddy. Mommy and I are just playing," the teenage son and daughter were holding on to their parents, and they, too, were crying. As I stumbled across the finish line of the story, mentioning the bust of Maggie on the parlor mantelpiece, I was emotionally drained. But by then, no one was watching me. They were watching the weeping man who was now approaching me. He extended his hand, and when I took it he said, "I am the great-great-grandson of William and Maggie Holladay."

It was such an incredibly powerful moment that the whole group gasped, and we all began crying. He went on to share his story, including family facts only a descendant could possibly know. Over generations, the family had moved west. His family was from Colorado and on their first visit to the East Coast. He knew his family came from North Carolina, but like with most people, the familial details diminish beyond a couple of generations. Yet the whole week, he and his family had pondered their roots and wondered if their ancestors could have ever visited this city or these beaches. And as it happened, on their last night, they decided to take the ghost walk. So when I said, "In 1889, William and Maggie Holladay," he was completely taken by surprise.

He retold the family story of Maggie's death and her ghostly appearance with William and the girls. He said the black dress was a favorite and the one she was buried in, though he was unsure why she was seen only from behind, as by all accounts she was a beautiful woman. His great-great-aunt Nannie always swore her mother's ghost was present with her while growing up. Sadly, his great-grandmother Marguerite could never speak of her mother, for she carried with her the guilt that she was the one responsible for her death.

The tour eventually ended, and the group slowly dispersed, the night's events weighing heavily on everyone. On the drive home, I reflected on my own life, remembering that moment when I was a little boy and my mother walked into my room to tell me my father had just died. I remember feeling so alone and vulnerable, so afraid of what life would be like without my father.

As I entered my home, my children greeted me, and I held them tight. They no doubt wondered why I was crying, afraid something was wrong. I told them everything was all right and sat with them on the couch next to my wife. I shared the story of what had just happened, and the kids grew wide-eyed. And as I watched their rapt attention and wonder, I thought, "I get it." As a parent, no matter what happens to you, you always want to be there for your children. And in this case, I believe that Maggie was.

# 4

# THE DUEL

*Though war is typically followed by peace, some men prefer to linger along the precipice of eternal hatred.*

Late one stormy summer evening in 1787, a half-drowned Englishman washed up on Wrightsville Beach. Rough seas had washed him overboard. A former naval officer during the American Revolution, he, like many British seamen, found his career ended with a peace treaty. Though four years had passed since the war's conclusion, for many on both sides of the Atlantic, the animosity and distrust of nearly eight years of fighting was simply too raw to begin healing.

When the Englishman was discovered, he was taken in by a veteran of the Revolutionary War, Major John Swann. Swann was a man of honor and believed in a military code that allowed for the utmost respect and treatment of a fellow officer, no matter what his allegiance. Swann opened his house to the Englishman until a time that funds could be secured to allow his safe return to British soil. Though many Wilmingtonians still wore the scars of British and Loyalist atrocities, they respected Major Swann's decision and showed the Englishman a common courtesy.

John Bradley, a local merchant, was also a veteran of the war. He had served with Major Swann, and the two were longtime friends. However, Bradley's recollections of Loyalists' depravities during the war, especially in the backcountry of North Carolina, were personal and vivid. In his eyes, there was no distinction between a Loyalist executing an innocent man and

The John Taylor Home currently sits on the site of the old dueling grounds. The area was once a large, open field, ideal for a pistol fight to the death. *Photo by John Hirchak.*

the British troops that provided the weaponry. So when he happened across his good friend Major Swann lending assistance to the former British naval officer, he felt betrayed.

"How," Bradley demanded of Swann, "can you aid an enemy you so gallantly fought against just years earlier?"

"My rancor toward British and Loyalist forces during the war is no secret," admitted Swan, "but the war is now over. It is time to put aside old hatred and rivalry."

Bradley was appalled. He argued that British and Loyalist conduct throughout the war was simply too heinous to forgive.

"But there is no evidence this man committed any such atrocities," Swann pointed out.

"Just as there is no evidence he did *not* commit such atrocities," Bradley retorted. "He is an admitted enemy!"

"He is not my enemy," Swann snapped. "Besides, he is a fellow officer, and I am honor-bound to provide him assistance."

Bradley scoffed at such a notion. "So you argue that your honor trumps our lifelong friendship?"

"I do not believe my honor trumps our friendship." Swann replied. "But I do believe that our friendship affords you the latitude to indulge my honor."

Bradley disagreed and continued to plead with Swann to remove the Englishman and send him on his way, but Swann refused, and the two men parted with ill feelings.

A few days later, the much-recovered Englishman unwittingly wandered into Bradley's store. Within seconds of walking through the door, he was immediately accosted by a vitriolic Bradley, who ordered him out of his business, attesting that he served neither Englishman nor Loyalist. The former officer wisely turned and left. However, shortly after this confrontation, Bradley publicly accused the Englishman of stealing a ring while in his shop.

The Englishman denied this claim, assuring Major Swann that Bradley had brusquely forced him to leave when he was no more than a few steps into his shop. Swann, understanding the Englishman's predicament of being nearly friendless and in a hostile environment, decided he would intervene on behalf of the former officer. However, when Swann arrived at his friend's shop, he found a livid Bradley fomenting outrage with a handful of men, demanding the Englishman be brought to justice.

At the sight of Major Swann, an enraged Bradley demanded to know if Swann had come to apologize for taking in the thieving Englishman. Swann was taken aback. He tried to reason with Bradley that the Englishman had assured him he had no opportunity to steal the ring. Bradley was incensed. He called the Englishman not only a thief but also a liar. Swann, feeling slightly affronted, assured Bradley that the Englishman was an honest and decent man and would neither steal nor lie.

John Bradley's temper overflowed. "You dare defend an enemy Englishman over a friend?" He roared.

"I am duty-bound to protect this officer," replied a stunned Major Swann. "I harbor no ill will toward him or any other Englishman."

"After all the British did against us, and the indignities they continue to carry out against our nation, you dare defend him over me?" Bradley shouted.

Eighteenth-century duels were typically fought to restore one's honor. Due to depth of field restraints, this image depicts the shooters standing very close to each other. Most duelists stood at least fifty feet apart. *Courtesy of Wikimedia Commons.*

"The British Crown may be at fault, but I cannot and will not hold an officer in need of assistance to blame for his king's arrogance," screamed Swann.

The exchange grew more heated until a furious Major Swann, feeling his honor was in question, rashly challenged Bradley to a duel. John Bradley abruptly accepted. Seconds, or representatives, were quickly selected, and by nightfall, the rules of the engagement had been settled. The two men, who just days earlier had been good friends, were now stubbornly committed to fight for their honor.

Contrary to popular belief, the intention of a duel wasn't necessarily to kill one's opponent so much as to gain satisfaction and restore one's honor. In the 1780s, pistol duels were typically fought with each party firing a single shot and, just as typically, missing, with the challenger stating he was thus "satisfied." The reason they often missed had to do with the poor shooting skills of many duelists at the time, the notorious inaccuracy of the weapons and the fact that, come the day of the duel, many friends realized the folly of their endeavor and intentionally missed. However, duels could also be fought with multiple shots fired—to first blood, mortal wounding or death.

Bradley, seething with anger, was prepared to fight to the death. Swann, an ace marksman, had some trepidation. Though he found it cowardly for two men to enter into a duel only to intentionally miss, he also did not wish to cause his friend harm.

On the morning of the duel, Swann, Bradley and their seconds met on the open field off Market Street, above North Fourth Street, on the present-day site of the John Taylor home (and Wilmington's first public library). The rules of the engagement were read aloud. The two men took their pistols and paced off the agreed upon distance. When the call came for the two men to take aim and fire, Major Swann quickly lifted his pistol and shot.

Blood and flesh exploded from Bradley's left upper thigh. The merchant cried out in pain, stumbling backward several steps before collapsing. At seeing his friend fall, Major Swann began to rush to his aid before realizing that the rules required him to hold his ground until his opponent either fired his pistol or was deemed incapable of firing. So Major Swann retook his ground and anxiously waited.

Earlier that morning, Major Swann had confessed to his second his plan to honorably relieve himself of his obligation without causing fatal harm to John Bradley. Swann told his second that he planned to shoot first in the hope of grazing his friend's hip with enough severity to lead to Bradley being incapable of shooting, thus ending the duel, saving his friend's life and restoring his honor. However, Swann now worried that the inaccuracy of the weapon had caused Bradley a fatal wound.

Then, after several tense minutes, John Bradley, with the aid of his second, restood his ground. Swann could see by the gaping wound in his friend's upper thigh that he had missed badly, hitting Bradley dead on. The damage indeed looked severe, but Swann was relieved to know he did not kill his friend. Swann, believing the duel would be called, was still in the act of studying his friend's wound when he realized Bradley had lifted his weapon as though to fire. Though a duelist would typically stand sideways in order to narrow his surface area, Swann, perhaps to communicate his true intention, stood square with Bradley and faced him full on. Bradley, trembling from pain and blood loss, took careful aim and fired.

Major Swann was dead before his body hit the ground. The lead ball struck him square in the face.

Subsequently, the Englishman vanished from Wilmington, perhaps signing on as crew on the next departing ship. John Bradley was arrested and placed on trial for the murder of Major John Swann. During the court's proceedings, Bradley learned of Swann's intention to cause a non-lethal wound in order to end the duel honorably. It was acknowledged that, should Swann have chosen to, he could have easily put a musket ball through

Bradley's heart. Bradley, on the other hand, unaware of Swann's objective, had fired to kill.

The court found the duel had been mutually agreed upon, and Bradley was set free. However, the court's finding of innocence was meaningless to Bradley. His remaining days were spent wallowing in regret, for he knew that when he raised his pistol and took aim at his friend, he had momentarily paused. In that brief moment, he should have recognized that Major John Swann was guilty of nothing more than being compassionate and forgiving; that he never failed to pursue the admirable path; and that, in his final moments on earth, he was prepared to stake his life on the premise that friendship should indeed trump honor. Instead, Bradley had pulled the trigger.

# 5

# PIRATES OF CAPE FEAR

I t's said that the first ship ever to take to sea was attacked and plundered by the pirates aboard the second ship that followed. Piracy is as old as maritime history itself, though most pirates remain nameless or are long forgotten. Today, the practice continues, with thousands of piratical acts committed annually. We refer to these modern-day pirates as thugs, warlords or gangsters. We don't cheer them when they raid a supertanker and murder innocent people. We want them captured or killed, for pirates are a loathsome lot. And yet, there was a small band of buccaneers who existed during a brief period of time and in a geographically narrow swath and are neither forgotten nor loathed. In fact, they are glorified. These brethren few collectively form our general conception of the "heroic" or "classic" pirate. Most of them plundered off the North Carolina coast or found safe harbor in Cape Fear country.

In the fourteenth century BC, the first recorded act of piracy occurred in the Aegean Sea. Soon, these marauding bands were pillaging throughout the Mediterranean. Julius Caesar himself suffered depredations at the hands of pirates. By AD 200, piracy was common in Asia, along most sea and river trade routes. In the fifteenth century, warring African, Asian and European nations authorized government-sponsored pirates known as privateers. By issuing letters of marque, nations granted legal right to raid and plunder enemy ships, ports and villages. Aside from the letters of marque, there is no real difference between a pirate and a privateer.

In 1522, the French privateer Jean Fleury took two Spanish galleons off the coast of the Azores. Much to the pirates' surprise, they found the galleons' holds brimming with Aztec gold, jewels and other valuables. This lone act of piracy was the impetus that brought pirates to the New World. Throughout the sixteenth and seventeenth centuries, the lucrative trade route between the Caribbean, the Americas and Europe exploded. With little military presence outside a port of call, save for the occasional naval escort that accompanied ships carrying the most valuable of cargo, merchant vessels were ripe for the plundering.

Pirates were generally welcome in most American ports. The colonists were hindered by Great Britain's unfair trade laws. Custom duties and royal taxes drove the price of imported goods higher while dragging down the value of exports. With colonists' diminished buying power, pirates helped fill a niche. Pirates, needing to sell their "hot" plunder quickly and with few questions asked, traded at a discount price and without penalty of tax. These savings were passed along to the colonists, who otherwise could scant afford to buy such fine housewares, jewelry or artwork. It's believed the vast majority of quality goods owned by colonists at this time were a result of pirate trade.

By 1690, not only were many colonists sympathetic to the pirates' cause, but they also invested in raids themselves. Colonists outfitted pirate ships to sail the Pirate Round, a sea route that started in America and led to Madagascar, the east coast of Africa and India before returning to the colonies. Along the route, these colonial pirates raided villages and plundered ships. Upon returning, the profit would be divided amongst investors. This practice continued up through the War of Spanish Succession (1701–13), known in the colonies as Queen Anne's War.

During this mainly European war, thousands of privateers were issued letters of marque. Investors bore the cost of outfitting the privateers, so warring nations didn't have to spend from their treasuries to build large navies. Privateers helped disrupt enemy commerce and were a drain on the enemy's navy, as military vessels were forced to protect merchant ships rather than engage in battle. Plunder was divided among the ship's crew, officers and investors. In addition to this newfound wealth, many privateers also experienced a level of freedom and equality they could never know in their home country.

By war's end, tens of thousands of merchant ships were either captured or sunk, and national treasuries were near depleted. In order to rebuild their respective economies, uninterrupted commerce was vital. So the peace treaty signed in 1713 was explicit: European nations were to cease all privateering activity. Overnight, thousands of well-trained privateers, having tasted the riches of plundering, and with no viable employment opportunities, turned to lives of piracy. Between 1714 and 1718, at the peak of what is considered the Golden Age of Piracy, over two thousand pirates were active off the coast of the Americas and the Caribbean. Unlike the pirates who preceded them, this lot was well trained by their foreign navies. They were hardened, used to being at sea for weeks, even months, at a time. They were audacious, willing to attack any vessel and blockade any port. And they were ruthless. The punishment for piracy was the same as the punishment for murder, so it made absolutely no difference how cruel one was while a-pirating.

This new breed of pirate discovered safe harbor and loads of plunder along the North Carolina and Cape Fear coast. With hundreds of miles of sparsely populated coastline dotted with scores of bays, inlets, rivers, creeks and channels, there were plenty of remote places to drop anchor and hide out. Sitting midway between the bustling ports of the Caribbean and New England, and on their oft-busy trading route, merchant ships were aplenty. Add to this scores of European-bound ships from the southern colonies, Central America, Hispaniola and the Greater Antilles that followed the Gulf Stream north to Frying Pan Shoals at the mouth of the Cape Fear River, before leaving the sight of land and following the northerly winds across the Atlantic, and the bounty seemed endless. It certainly didn't hurt to have a governor who profited greatly from his relationship to known pirates and was more than willing to turn a blind eye to these gentlemen of fortune.

## A Pirate's Life for Me?

Piracy was not as glorious as Hollywood would like for you to believe. The characters portrayed by Errol Flynn and Johnny Depp couldn't be further from the truth. A pirate's life was hard, violent and, with few exceptions, quite short. Battle, shipwreck, tavern brawls, scurvy and tropical disease killed most pirates. For those who managed to survive such travails, their fate was a short drop and a sudden stop, for piracy was punishable by hanging.

The image of a smartly dressed pirate burying a treasure chest overflowing with doubloons and pieces of eight, only to reclaim it later with the use of a pirate map, isn't exactly accurate. Yes, pirates did value maps, but strictly for navigational purposes. In fact, there is no known instance of a pirate actually using a treasure map. The truth is that X never marked the spot. The burying of treasure is also mainly myth. Though there are two known instances of pirates burying their loot, they typically wanted to sell or trade their plunder quickly. And contrary to popular belief, booty was typically neither gold nor silver. Typical pirate swag included sugar, spices, fabric, tobacco and the like. Medicines, wood-working tools, canvas, rope, cookware, food and water were also sought after. And most pirates remained penniless, as they were apt to quickly blow their share on wenches, rum and gambling.

Aside from Stede Bonnet, very few pirates actually forced anyone to "walk the plank." It was far easier to simply throw victims overboard. They also preferred smaller, swifter ships with shallow drafts that allowed for a quick escape, which was a pirate's best defense. A minimal draft allowed access to shallow marshes and inlets, where larger ships were precluded. This was important when it came time to careen the pirate ship. Careening took upward of a week and involved pulling or tipping the vessel over and exposing half the hull. Planking damaged by rot or marine worms was replaced, adzes were used to hack off barnacles and the hull was treated with tallow and sulfur. During this slow, backbreaking process, pirates were at their most exposed to attack or capture, so the smaller the ship, the smaller the hull and the quicker the repairs.

The original pirate's flag was made of red cloth and known as the "blood flag." When flown, it indicated that the attacking ship did not honor typical rules of engagement and consisted of outlaws. It also conveyed there would be little or no mercy to those who tried to flee or fight. Over time, pirates began crudely painting a white skull and femurs, or crossbones, on their flags, which was later referred to as the "Jolly Roger." By the Golden Age of Piracy, the red flag was replaced with the darker, more sinister "black" flag. The pirate captains of this era began to individualize their flags, decorating the fabric with their own unique logos as a sort of personal calling card. But whatever flag a pirate flew, he waited until he was almost upon his prey before unfurling it, for even a hint that an approaching vessel was a pirate ship was enough to make any merchant ship flee.

An interesting truism, certainly highlighted in Disney's *Pirates of the Caribbean* movies, was the Articles of Piracy (also known as the Pirate Code or the Articles of Agreement). In the class-based societies of the sixteenth, seventeenth and early eighteenth centuries, there was practically no hope of rising above one's station. If you were born poor, you died poor, and for the most part, the vast population was controlled by lords and overseers who maintained the status quo. During this time in world history, democracy, equality and freedom were hard to come by. Except, that is, aboard a pirate ship.

Flags of the most notorious Cape Fear pirates. *From top, left to right*: the Jolly Roger, Edward Low, "Calico" Jack Rackham, Stede "the Gentleman Pirate" Bonnet, Blackbeard and the "Blood Flag." *Illustration courtesy of Margot Beberaggi.*

Most ships had their own versions of the Articles of Piracy. The document spelled out discipline, the division of plunder and compensation for a pirate's injuries. The articles typically stipulated that the captain was to be elected by the crew in a democratic manner, with one vote per crewmate. And though the captain was responsible for day-to-day decisions, any important affairs were to be voted on by the crew. If a captain proved to be incompetent or concerned only with his own fame or fortune, he could simply be voted out of office.

In addition to everyone having an equal voice, the pirates also split all captured booty in a fair manner. Crew typically received one share apiece, while the captain, quartermaster and a few other select officers received double shares as compensation for their extra responsibilities. And so, whether English, African, French, Spanish, Native American or Dutch, everyone profited and received equal treatment, unlike aboard the typical naval or merchant ships of their day. So when ships were captured and the subjugated crew was offered the opportunity to turn pirate, to free themselves from authority, to have fair treatment and equal voice and to have a chance at riches otherwise unattainable, many law-abiding sailors eagerly accepted.

This is not to say that life aboard a pirate ship was peaceful paradise. It wasn't. The motley crew was composed of men from society's lower social strata who shared a common criminality. To keep order amongst their fellow rabble, discipline was strictly enforced. Simple violations, such as failing to pull one's weight, were dealt with by the quartermaster, typically through whipping. More serious infractions were dealt with by consent of the crew. For example, if a fellow pirate was caught stealing from a crewmate—a very serious accusation aboard a pirate ship—the offending pirate would be tried before a jury of his peers. If the defendant was found guilty, the jury would pronounce a sentence that might include a simple fine, whipping, marooning, keelhauling or death. Keelhauling was done by running a long rope beneath the ship's hull and attaching one end to the pirate's ankles and the other to his wrists. The guilty wretch would then be thrown overboard and, like a human trinket on a rope bracelet, dragged back and forth across the razor-sharp, barnacle-encrusted hull. The salt water would burn the torn flesh, and the fortunate would die quickly. Of course, the crew also had the option of simplifying one's sentence by casting the offender overboard.

## The Most Notorious of the Scourges

Though thousands of pirates plundered ships off the Cape Fear coast or sought shelter along our shore during the Golden Age of Piracy, most remain nameless and are of little consequence. A few, like Charles Bellamy, Robert Deal, William Fly and Christopher Moody, were, in their time, known by name and their ships feared, though for the most part they and their deeds are long forgotten. A few others achieved a slightly higher level of notoriety, and their names are remembered to this day.

Captain William Lewis had a career spanning nine years, a considerable time for any pirate. He often boasted that his fortitude came from the devil himself. This boasting would lead to his eventual demise. While off the Cape Fear coast, in pursuit of a seemingly slower ship, a lucky cannon shot blew off his foremast. As his ship quickly slowed, Lewis climbed the top mast and began pulling out his hair, screaming, "Good devil, take this till I come!" Suddenly, his ship gained speed, overcoming and capturing the prize. However, later that night, his disconcerted crew, convinced Captain Lewis had summoned Satan to do his bidding, murdered him in his sleep, believing he had become too intimate with the devil.

Captain George Lowther sailed with some of the most vicious pirates of the time but is probably best remembered for his cowardice during times of engagement. While off the Cape Fear coast, he attacked a smaller ship. However, when the smaller ship failed to surrender and instead turned to engage in battle, a shaken Captain Lowther and his crew beached their ship and swam to shore, spending the winter hiding out on our rugged coastline. The next spring, he returned to piracy and again was engaged in battle by a smaller vessel. He again escaped ashore and was later found to have put a ball of lead through his head rather than risk capture and hanging.

## CHARLES VANE

Captain Charles Vane was not lacking in self-confidence. He was also arrogant, lucky, sadistic and, if the moment necessitated, a coward—a not-so-frowned-upon trait for those wishing to fight another day. He had a reputation for cruelty, often promising mercy to a merchant crew if they surrendered and then, once disarmed, torturing and murdering them. Vane also showed a willingness to ignore the Pirate Code if it suited him, going so far as to cheat his own crew of plunder. He was fearless in that he was unafraid to drop anchor off major ports and rob all incoming and outgoing merchant ships. His reign of terror lasted three years; however, it was during his last twelve months at sea that he truly brought fear into the hearts of many. During this last year, the mere rumor of his presence off the coast would bring commerce to a halt.

Trained as a privateer, one of his first acts of piracy was as a crewman of Captain Henry Jennings. In 1715, Jennings raided a Spanish camp, making off with £85,000 in silver and gold. Shortly thereafter, Vane procured a small sloop and began his career as a pirate captain. Though his initial home base was at the abandoned colony of New Providence in the Bahamas, he plundered from Nassau to New York.

In September 1717, King George offered a blanket pardon to all pirates who vowed to return to an honest life. Vane scoffed at the idea. What proceeded was a whirlwind of raiding, plundering, torture and murder. In February 1718, Vane was stopped by the HMS *Phoenix* and boarded. Vane claimed he had been en route to Nassau to accept the king's pardon. Amazingly he was granted his freedom, though he did lose his ship. He immediately returned to piracy, assembling a new crew of some of the worst piratical cutthroats available, including Edward England and "Calico Jack" Rackham. They set sail for the lucrative coast of North Carolina.

Though Captain Charles Vane was an arrogant man, he also cherished the act of cowardice, if necessary, in order to live to fight another day. *Courtesy of Wikimedia Commons.*

Throughout the spring, this new band of thieves was productive, capturing scores of vessels. Vane continued to trade up to larger and larger ships until he was in command of a twelve-gun brigantine he christened *Ranger*, a name he used for all subsequent ships under his charge. During this stay, his bold and often bloody attacks helped grow his legend. He soon captured a twenty-gun French ship, and with more than enough firepower, his pirate armada sailed for Nassau. He soon controlled the port, flying a pirate flag from atop the small fort near the harbor entrance.

When ships of the Royal Navy arrived to retake Nassau, Vane fired on them. Realizing he held a tenuous position, he waited until nightfall, set his twenty-gun ship afire and sent it toward the Royal Navy line. He hoped his unmanned ship would reach the navy line and then explode; however, the navy quickly cut its lines and dispersed. With a smaller, swifter six-gun sloop, Vane slipped between the scattering naval ships, boldly firing a single cannon shot in the governor's direction, vowing he would return.

Vane soon acquired two more ships and, with a sizable crew, dropped anchor off Charleston Harbor in September 1718. He captured several ships before sailing north to Cape Fear, where he continued to plunder. Later that month, he hooked up with Blackbeard on Ocracoke Island for a weeklong piratical blowout: drinking, gambling and womanizing. Vane tried to convince Blackbeard to join him in another attack on Nassau, but Blackbeard refused. Vane soon set sail for New York.

In November 1718, Vane engaged with a large French navy warship. Severely outgunned, he decided to flee. "Calico Jack" Rackham was livid, accusing Vane of cowardice, which resulted in Vane being deposed and Rackham being voted captain. Vane was sent his way and attempted a return to piracy. Before getting far, his ship wrecked in a storm, and he was captured. Shortly thereafter, he was hanged for piracy.

# Edward Low

Edward Low was born in London to a family of thieves. He had a quick temper and wasn't afraid of a fight. He loved to gamble but was a known cheat. As a young man, he learned to pick pockets and burglarize homes. His older brother was actually hanged for burglary. At a young age, Low moved to the colonies, bouncing around before settling in Boston. He started a family and tried his hand at an honest trade; however, after the tragic loss of a child and his young wife, he turned to piracy. Though his career lasted only two years, he was, without a doubt, the most bloodthirsty pirate of the Golden Age.

Low sailed under the flag of Captain George Lowther, who had a knack for turning desperate men into ferocious pirates. It didn't take Lowther long to recognize that Low was insane, possibly psychotic. Perhaps out of fear, Lowther decided to offer Low a six-gun brigantine and forty-four crewmen, and the two went their separate ways. During his time as captain, Low covered great distances in search of plunder. His range included the Carolina and Cape Fear coast, New England, Nova Scotia, Newfoundland, the Azores, the Canary Islands, Cape Verde, Brazil, Central America and the greater Caribbean Sea.

A 1734 engraving showing Captain Edward Low as the sole survivor following the sinking of his ship during a hurricane. *Courtesy of Library of Congress.*

Initially, Captain Low's wrath was reserved for New Englanders, for whom he held a strong hatred (though over time, no ship under any flag was safe). One of his favorite torture techniques involved tightly weaving a rope through a captive's individual fingers before tying off their wrists. He would then set the rope alight. The tight weave caused the rope to smolder and slowly burn the flesh off the victim's hands. He also enjoyed cutting the masts off New England ships and setting the crew adrift with no food or water, making for a slow, painful death. Later, he grew fond of chaining crews to their decks before setting their ships on fire. In fact, of the hundreds of ships Low captured during his career, including a staggering thirteen in one day, many were sent to the bottom of the sea.

As time passed, Low's rage grew more intense. With capture by Low inevitable, a Portuguese captain dropped overboard a bag containing over eleven thousand gold moidores rather than surrender them to a pirate. Low cut off the captain's lips, cooked them and made the man eat them while still burning hot. He then murdered the entire crew. On a separate occasion, he had two Portuguese captives hoisted up to the yardarm and then repeatedly dropped until they were dead. He burned a Frenchman alive, stating the man was greasy and would fry well. Despite what was already a savage résumé, the worst was yet to come.

During the torture of captives from a recently plundered ship, a crewmate accidently slashed Low across the face, through the mouth, from cheek to cheek. Low exploded in anger, killing men wantonly. He was in such a furor that the ship's surgeon refused to help him. So Low, delirious with rage and with the aid of a mirror, stitched his own face back together. He botched the job and was left grossly mutilated. This ushered in a level of atrocity never before seen in the pirating world. On the next ship he captured, he personally murdered fifty-three Spaniards, running them through with his sword. He also began a practice of cutting off the ears, noses and lips of captives, forcing them to literally eat their own faces. As word of these horrors spread, cries came from both sides of the Atlantic to capture or kill this psychopath.

Several British warships were dispatched to try and capture Low. At the time, Low had two ships: the *Fancy*, which he captained, and the *Ranger*. While off the coast of North Carolina, Low mistook one of the ships sent to capture him, the HMS *Greyhound*, for a merchant ship. When Low attacked, the twenty-gun *Greyhound* opened fire. Both the *Fancy* and *Ranger* briefly returned fire before deciding to flee. A three-hour running battle ensued, and though the *Greyhound* managed to dismast the *Fancy*, it escaped. The abandoned *Ranger* was boarded, and hand-to-hand combat ensued before the surviving pirates surrendered. The entire crew of the *Ranger* was ultimately hanged for piracy, but Low and the *Fancy*, laden with £150,000 in gold, escaped.

Infuriated at the loss of the *Ranger*, Low tortured the captain of the next ship he captured before finishing him off with a pistol shot to the head. The crew was set adrift in a small boat with no provisions. The captain of Low's next prize was decapitated. From the following two ships, Low scalped some captives and disemboweled others. His savagery became so extreme that his own crew began to refuse his orders. And then, suddenly and without explanation, the story of Captain Edward Low mercifully ends. Whether he was lost at sea, murdered by his own fearful crew or, as some speculate, retired in Brazil a wealthy man to spend his remaining days ashore, the truth is, his fate is unknown. But whatever the cause of his disappearance, few wept over his loss.

## Calico, Bonny and Read

There is little known of the early life of the pirate known as Anne Bonny. It's believed she was born in Ireland. Her family arrived in the Carolinas while Anne was still a young girl. Her father, after a failed attempt at law, turned to a much more profitable career as a merchant. Her mother died before Anne's thirteenth birthday. This may have led to Anne's violent temper, which resulted in her stabbing a servant with a table knife. She went on to marry John Bonny, a poor, small-time pirate and sailor, and the two settled in Nassau. John Bonny abruptly turned pirate informant, which didn't sit well with Anne. She began visiting local taverns, seeking out and consorting with known pirates. This is when she met the notorious "Calico Jack" Rackham, and the two fell in love.

Rackham was called "Calico Jack" because of his propensity for wearing calico fabric: a cloth of small, recurring floral patterns that's typically very colorful. He began his career as quartermaster under Captain Charles Vane, becoming captain after Vane was deposed by his crew. Some of his first acts of piracy as captain involved taking prizes off the Cape Fear, Carolina and Bermudan coasts. It was off Cape Fear where Rackham captured several impressive prizes, which helped build his reputation as a daring and capable leader.

From Cape Fear, Rackham sailed for the Caribbean, plundering ships along the way. In Port Royal, he stole a merchant ship, its holds bulging with valuable cargo. Unfortunately, he seized the ship within view of shore, and several of the port's enraged merchants decided to give chase. Unaware of his pursuers, Rackham anchored his prize off Isla de los Pinos, Cuba. The angry merchants retook their ship. However, Rackham and most of his crew were ashore, so they managed to escape.

Rackham didn't stay on land long. He stole a small sloop and sailed for a small Cuban port, where he proceeded to refit the ship to meet his pirating needs. While in port, a patrolling Spanish warship entered the harbor with a captured English sloop in tow. The Spaniards spotted Rackham's pirate ship, but with an ebb tide and dusk approaching, they decided to drop anchor at the harbor entrance and wait until dawn before attacking. Rackham understood his predicament. At nightfall, he and his crew noiselessly rowed small boats out to the captured English sloop and quietly overpowered the Spanish guards. At dawn, the Spanish warship rained cannon fire down on the docked pirate sloop. With the warship distracted, Rackham, aboard the much faster English sloop, escaped before the Spaniards had time to react.

Rackham continued on to Nassau and accepted a royal pardon offered by Governor Woode Rogers. It was during his brief interlude as a pardoned man that Rackham met Anne Bonny. However, shortly after their illicit affair began, Anne's husband found out about it and petitioned the governor, who ordered Anne to be whipped. Rackham offered to buy her through divorce, but she was against the idea of being sold like an animal. Instead, the two, along with a newly formed crew, stole a sloop and reverted to piracy.

While a-pirating, Anne became pregnant with Rackham's child. While Rackham remained at sea to continue his piratical ways, Anne was put ashore in Cuba, where she gave birth to their son. While recuperating, Anne met a dashing young pirate to whom she took an instant liking. Anne began to make advances on this young man, who soon revealed he was actually a cross-dressing Englishwoman named Mary Read. The two became fast friends.

Mary Read was born an illegitimate child and had been forced by her mother to dress as a boy following the death of her older brother. This disguise allowed the family to continue receiving financial support from her grandparents. While a young teenager, she continued the ruse of dressing like a man, fighting for the British during the War for Spanish Succession. After the war, she married and settled in the Netherlands, where she and her husband operated an inn. Following his untimely death, and while still a very young woman, Mary decided to set sail for the New World. To gain

A copper engraving of Anne Bonny and Mary Read. Original engraving by Benjamin Cole (1695–1766). *Courtesy of Wikimedia Commons.*

work, she resumed her male persona. However, on the voyage to the West Indies, the ship she was on was captured by pirates, and Read, like other male captives, was forced to turn flag. When the king's pardon of 1717 was granted, she and her fellow crew accepted and received a commission to privateer. Soon after, the dissatisfied crew mutinied, and she joined them, once again returning to a life of piracy. It was during this period, while ashore in Cuba, that she met Anne Bonny.

When Rackham returned for Anne, she convinced him to take this strapping young man on as crew. Rackham agreed. However, unaware that Read was really a woman, he grew jealous of all the attention Anne lavished upon this new crewman. One night, he threatened to slit the man's throat, and Anne let him in on the secret. Rackham agreed to allow Read to remain aboard, and the three of them continued a-pirating. Though their time together lasted only a few months, Anne Bonny and Mary Read assisted in the plunder of numerous ships. Many captives who fought against the duo were later surprised to learn they were women, claiming they were braver than their male counterparts. Mary is known to have killed at least one man, possibly more.

In a quiet Jamaican cove, their ship dropped anchor, and the pirates took to drinking. That night, an English warship crept upon them, attacking at first light. Most of the crew, including Calico Jack, was too drunk to fight and fled to the temporary safety of the hold. Anne, Mary and one other crewmate fought off the military sailors, cursing the cowardice of their fellow pirates. Mary angrily fired a shot into the hold, killing one pirate and wounding another. Though Anne and Mary were willing to fight to the death, the sailors soon overcame them, and the rest of the pirates sheepishly surrendered.

Anne and Mary both claimed to be with child, which was enough to put their executions on hold. Rackham had no such claim, and he, like the rest of his crew, was sentenced to hanging. On the way to the gallows, Rackham asked to see Anne, who refused to look at him. As he was being led out, she said, "If you had fought like a man, you would not have to be hanged like a dog." Minutes later, Rackham and his crew were hanged like dogs. Mary Read died in prison, either of fever or during childbirth. Anne Bonny's end is a mystery. There is no record of her execution. It's believed that her father, a wealthy merchant in the Carolinas with many contacts throughout the Caribbean, was able to buy her release. She returned to the Carolinas, where she remarried, had several children and went on to lead a quiet life.

During this Golden Age of Piracy, each of these aforementioned pirates reached an exceptional level of notoriety. Their names and deeds were well known on both sides of the Atlantic, and they each encapsulate a piece of what it meant to be a pirate: the bold fearlessness of Charles Vane, the ruthless ferocity of Edward Low and the cunningness and flair of Calico Jack Rackham. Anne Bonny and Mary Read stand alone as the only two women found guilty of piracy during this Golden Age. And yet, in the upper echelons of notorious pirates, two stand above all others.

## Teach and Bonnet

Edward Teach and Stede Bonnet coexisted for much of their short careers, sailing together under one flag. Their legendary deeds are near mythical, and they, more than any other of this era, form our collective image of a "pirate." Their impact on North Carolina and the Cape Fear coast cannot be overstated. But the paths that led them together, and to our shores, couldn't have been more different.

Edward Teach's real name will probably never be known. It is simply an alias he bestowed on himself. During the War of Spanish Succession, Teach enjoyed the life of a privateer, where he honed his sailing and

A pirate attack was a risky venture for all involved. The life of a pirate was typically violent and short. *The Buccaneers* by Frederick Judd Waugh. *Courtesy of Library of Congress.*

plundering skills. After the war, Teach briefly tried his hand at honest wages before signing on with pirate captain Benjamin Hornigold in 1716. Teach quickly proved himself ambitious, strong, intelligent and fearless. By early 1717, he had earned his own ship and crew and sailed aside Captain Hornigold.

Throughout the early part of 1717, Hornigold and Teach plundered numerous ships off North Carolina and along the colonial coast. The two men were bold, but contrary to modern belief, they were not brutes. Teach specifically never showed any cruelty to his captives. But in the days of Charles Vane and Edward Low, all pirates were seen as murderous barbarians.

Major Stede Bonnet was born to a wealthy landowning family in Barbados. He was educated and well respected. Upon his father's death, he inherited a four-hundred-acre farm, a considerable size at the time. He served in the Barbados militia, where he received the rank of major. He married and fathered four children. At twenty-nine years of age, he represented a true life of leisure. However, in the spring of 1717, under the guise of building a ship in order to trade with nearby islands, Bonnet decided to sail away from his wealth, status and family. His friends thought he suffered from a disorder of the mind or simply tired of the dull life of a wealthy landowner, but the truth was, he could no longer tolerate his nagging wife.

With no knowledge of the sea, Bonnet's path to piracy was unlike any who preceded him. Where most pirates either mutiny or steal their first ship, Bonnet paid to have a sixty-ton sloop built, which he later named *Revenge*, and equipped it with six guns. He enlisted a crew, paying them a fair wage rather than a share of the plunder, as most all other pirate crews expected. Since he knew nothing of seafaring, he hired a knowledgeable quartermaster and officers. Then one evening, with no hint of his departure, he weighed anchor and made for the Cape Fear coast and the busy southern shipping lanes.

For a pirate with no experience, he ran a tight ship. He was quick to punish insubordination for even the slightest infraction. Whatever he lacked in experience, he more than made up for in courage. He was willing to attack any ship, no matter its size. Within a few weeks of turning pirate, he captured and plundered four vessels. With early success, his reputation spread, and though he preferred the alias Captain Thomas, his well-bred gentlemanly demeanor soon led him to be known as "the Gentleman Pirate."

Bonnet continued to capture ships from New York to the Carolinas. At the entrance to Charleston Harbor, he took two ships. He relieved the smaller vessel of its cargo before releasing it with both crews. He towed the larger ship back to the Cape Fear coast. In a hidden inlet, he plundered the larger ship before dismantling it and using the timbers to make repairs to his own sloop.

Despite these successes, his lack of seafaring experience failed to win over his crew's respect. As the murmurs of discontent rumbled aboard Bonnet's ship, he set sail south, where he encountered a Spanish man-o-war. A brutal battle ensued in which half of Bonnet's crew was killed or wounded. In addition, Bonnet suffered serious wounds, and his ship was badly damaged but not captured. He limped into the port of Nassau, where he refitted his ship, increasing his guns to twelve, and took on additional crew. It was here, in September 1717, that Bonnet first encountered Teach and Hornigold.

Hornigold revealed to Bonnet and Teach that he planned to go his separate way, retiring shortly thereafter. Bonnet and Teach struck up a friendship and decided to sail together. Bonnet, still recovering from wounds received while battling the Spanish man-o-war, agreed to temporarily cede command of the *Revenge* to Teach. Though some argue Teach took control of the *Revenge* in a more forceful manner, the fact remains that, at the time, Stede was physically incapable of commanding his own ship. Regardless, the influence both pirates had on each other, and on pirate lore, was significant and should not be downplayed. They would spend most of their remaining days a-pirating together.

By then, Teach had completed his new persona. Around his tall, broad-shouldered physique, he created a frightening, unforgettable figure meant to strike fear in the hearts of man. Before battle, he would braid his long, thick beard in pigtails, tying off the ends with small, colorful ribbon. He wore a snug-fitting, wide-brimmed hat, under which he inserted strands of slow-burning cannon matches, allowing them to dangle about his head. The incessant smoke of the slow-burning matches infiltrated his hair and beard, giving the appearance that his head was on fire. He donned black, knee-length boots and dark-colored clothing, which he topped with a brightly colored silk or velvet long coat. Across his broad torso draped a bandolier that held half a dozen pistols, loaded and cocked for the ready. He wore a brightly colored sash across his waist, stuffed with cutlasses and knives. To complete his devilish transformation, he dropped the alias Edward Teach and began going by the name Blackbeard.

In September, Blackbeard and Bonnet sailed north to ply the waters between Cape Fear and Delaware Bay. Within weeks, they had taken over a dozen ships laden with valuable cargo. Their successful run carried through October, when, late in the month, a captain from one of the captured ships reported seeing Bonnet aboard the *Revenge* in a much-weakened state, still recovering from his wounds. In November, the pirates returned to the Caribbean, and on November 17, they attacked a two-hundred-ton ship nearly one hundred miles out from Martinique. Their prey initially tried to fight off the pirates. However, after Blackbeard fired two broadsides and several rounds of musket fire, the ship quickly surrendered. Blackbeard took possession of this larger ship, renaming it *Queen Anne's Revenge*, and outfitted it with forty guns. By this time, the pirates were in possession of three ships, over 150 men and nearly sixty cannons. Each subsequent attack helped cement Blackbeard's reputation as the most daring pirate on the high seas. Though Blackbeard intentionally created an image of a crazed, murderous pirate, there is no record of him ever torturing or killing a single captive. Indeed, he may very well have been the least murderous pirate of this era.

By late December, Bonnet had recovered from his wounds and resumed command of the *Revenge*. Shortly thereafter, the two pirates parted ways and continued to plunder in proximity to each other. Though Blackbeard and Bonnet exhibited fearlessness in battle and had similar success, Bonnet's crew continued to doubt his abilities as captain. After failing to capture

One of the most widely used images of Edward Teach, following his transformation into the dreaded pirate Blackbeard. *Courtesy of Wikimedia Commons.*

a four-hundred-ton merchant ship in March 1718, Bonnet sought out and relinquished control of the *Revenge* to the better-able Blackbeard. With a force of three vessels, they captured a merchant ship and persuaded the captain, David Herriot, Israel Hands and several other crewmen to join them. The pirates, now spread across four ships, numbered more than three hundred.

With warmer weather upon them, the pirates decided to sail to North Carolina. It was time for careening, and the inlets along and near the Cape Fear River, Wrightsville and Topsail Beaches, the Pamlico and Albemarle Sounds and the Cowan River were favorite hideouts. Teach's Hole, aside the island of Ocracoke, is so named because it was a preferred anchorage of Blackbeard's. However, before arriving at the Cape Fear coast, they decided to engage in one final bold act of piracy.

In late May, Blackbeard's four-ship flotilla dropped anchor off the mouth of Charleston Harbor, one of the southern colonies' most vital ports. Over six days, he took nine ships, including the port's pilot boat, a slave ship, a vessel carrying £6,000 in gold and a ship carrying Samuel Wragg, a member of Governor Johnson's Council of the Province of the Carolinas. Blackbeard, in need of medical supplies for his crew, decided to ransom Wragg and his other hostages. Several crewmen boldly sailed one of the captured ships into the harbor accompanied by a captive named Mr. Marks as proof of the hostage situation and to ensure that Blackbeard's threat was communicated properly. If the city failed to deliver the supplies in two days, Blackbeard would enter the harbor, set fire to the remaining ships and behead the hostages.

Blackbeard and his eight ships (four of his own and four captured) dropped anchor fifteen miles off the coast and waited. On the third day, a message was delivered from Mr. Marks explaining their boat had capsized while en route to shore, delaying their arrival. Blackbeard agreed to a two-day extension. After another two days passed without word, Blackbeard met with Bonnet and several of their officers, deciding to sail into Charleston Harbor to help usher things along. When his ships entered the harbor, panic ensued. Before any ships were set afire, Mr. Marks and the remaining pirates returned with chests of medicine valued at £300 to £400. Mr. Marks explained that the additional delay was due to the fact that Blackbeard's pirates were off on a drunken rampage and proved difficult to corral. Blackbeard, true to his word, released the hostages, short their fine clothing, and returned them to shore mostly naked. The humiliation brought upon the people of Charleston would not be forgotten.

The pirate fleet sailed north, arriving at Topsail Inlet in mid-June. Unbeknownst to Bonnet, Blackbeard, under the guise of his ships needing careening, intentionally grounded the *Queen Anne's Revenge* and a second ship. Suddenly, the pirate fleet was reduced to two ships: the *Revenge* and the *Adventure*. As the captains discussed what should be done, Blackbeard, according to plan, let it be known that the king had extended his pardon. Blackbeard, believing he could trust Governor Charles Eden of North Carolina, wished to accept it. He encouraged Bonnet and several of his men to set out for Bath, North Carolina. When Bonnet and his crew arrived in Bath, they surrendered and were granted the king's pardon. In addition to the pardon, Bonnet's governor-promised letters of marque were waiting for him in Saint Thomas, which would allow him to return to privateering against the French. With the promise of a commission and a sizable share of plunder waiting for him, Bonnet and his crew eagerly returned to Topsail Inlet. There, he discovered Blackbeard had outwitted him.

While Bonnet was busy seeking his pardon in Bath, Blackbeard was busy transferring all the stolen booty and stocks from the *Revenge* to the *Adventure*. Blackbeard was sure to make his intent to sail to Ocracoke Inlet well known before driving off a large number of crew who fled to shore, fearing the double-dealing captain. With a crew of forty, he headed north and then quickly marooned twenty-five more men on a spit of sand miles off the mainland. With a much-reduced crew, he would retain an even larger share of the plunder. He then deceptively sailed north before changing course, arriving in Bath, from where Bonnet had departed just a day or so earlier, and accepted the king's pardon.

When Bonnet discovered Blackbeard's duplicity, he flew into a rage. He rescued the aptly named *Revenge* and recovered some of the crew who had fled ashore. Understanding Blackbeard intended to careen his ship in Ocracoke Inlet, Bonnet made pursuit, rescuing the twenty-five marooned men along the way. While Bonnet searched Ocracoke and the surrounding islands, Blackbeard took up residence on the Bath Creek at Plum Point, close to Governor Eden's home and Tobias Knight, the governor's secretary and a member of the council. For the better part of two months, he would remain there, living the life of a distinguished, wealthy gentleman.

Unable to locate the elusive Blackbeard, lacking the funds and stores to make the journey to Saint Thomas to claim his commission and in the midst of hurricane season (making any journey to the Caribbean a risky one), Bonnet was forced to return to a life of piracy. In an attempt to mask his identity, he renamed the *Revenge* the *Royal James*, though this deception was short-lived, as word soon spread that the Gentleman Pirate had forsaken the king's pardon. Off the coast of North Carolina, Bonnet plundered several

Stede "the Gentleman Pirate" Bonnet, as depicted from a popular woodcut of the era. *Courtesy of Wikimedia Commons.*

ships before turning north to Delaware Bay. In early August, he pillaged eleven ships, keeping the last two for use in repairing the *Royal James*, which was badly in need of careening. He returned to North Carolina, dropping anchor on the Cape Fear River, in what is today known as Bonnet's Creek. His intent was to wait out hurricane season before sailing on to Saint Thomas, still believing his commission awaited him.

By the end of August, Blackbeard had bored of being a gentleman and quietly returned to piracy. Using Ocracoke as a home base, he took several small prizes off the coast of North Carolina. In September, he captured two French ships near Delaware Bay. Transporting the cargo onto one and releasing the other, he returned to Bath with the French ship in tow, making the ridiculous claim that he had found the ship adrift with no crewmen present. The governor convened a vice-admiralty court, with Tobias Knight as judge, and the French ship was deemed a legitimate prize. Sixty hogsheads of sugar were awarded to the governor and twenty to Knight, while Blackbeard and his crew were free to sell all that remained. Under the pretense that the ship was no longer seaworthy, and wishing to rid himself of the evidence, he towed the ship to sea and burned it to the water line.

The governors of both South Carolina and Virginia were fed up with the pirate scourge. News that Blackbeard and Bonnet were offered safe harbor in North Carolina infuriated them. South Carolina was considering sending out ships to try and capture these and other pirates when a new threat emerged. Captain Charles Vane, looking to emulate the success of Blackbeard a few months earlier, began plundering ships off Charleston Harbor. Though Vane succeeded in capturing only a few vessels, his appearance was the incentive the governor of South Carolina needed to move forward. He authorized two eight-gun sloops, the flagship *Henry* and the *Sea Nymph*, with a total crew of 130, under the command of Colonel William Rhett, to capture Vane.

Vane had been overheard by one of his captives claiming he planned on careening his ships in an inlet south of Charleston. However, after an extensive search, Rhett failed to locate the pirate and decided to venture north. On September 26, he arrived at the mouth of the Cape Fear River. Knowing this to be a favorite pirate haunt, he sailed upriver, where he spotted three masts poking through the trees. Convinced he had discovered Vane, Rhett prepared to attack. However, before he could engage, his flagship ran aground. Realizing it would be dark before his ship would refloat, he was forced to wait until dawn before proceeding.

In the meantime, Bonnet spotted the two grounded ships downriver but mistook them for merchantmen ripe for plunder. When night fell, he sent a few small boats to capture them, but they returned with news that the ships were armed and preparing for battle. Rather than flee upriver, Bonnet decided to wait until dawn and make a fight for the open sea. Spread out over three ships, he ordered all forty-six of his men aboard the larger *Royal James*. Through the night, Bonnet and Rhett drove their crews hard, preparing for what both knew was likely a battle to the death.

As dawn broke on September 27, Bonnet weighed anchor, raised the blood flag and set course for Rhett's ships, which by then were afloat and ready for battle. The *Royal James* quickly opened fire with cannons and muskets, and the *Henry* and *Sea Nymph* returned fire, beginning the Battle of Cape Fear River. Bonnet tried to break for the sea, but Rhett, anticipating just such a move, closed in. A running battle ensued with the three vessels exchanging broadsides. The *Sea Nymph* suddenly and violently ran aground and was removed from battle. The *Royal James* and *Henry* continued downriver, exchanging fire before Rhett, for the second time, grounded the *Henry*. Bonnet attempted to skirt the western shore and escape, but his ship also ran aground.

Though the *Sea Nymph* was well out of range, the *Royal James* and the *Henry* remained within pistol-shot range of each other. They both careened in the same direction, the *Henry* canted with its deck fully exposed to the *Royal James*, which canted with its hull facing the *Henry*. The pirates, in a better position, unleashed a blistering amount of cannon and musket fire across the *Henry*'s deck. Rhett's exposed crew returned fire, but without the same efficacy. Bonnet, pistol in hand, marched back and forth threatening to kill any crew member who displayed cowardice. But the pirates' spirits were high, for they felt confident they had the upper hand. Taunts were shouted back and forth between the two ships. After five hours, the tide started to rise. Still, all three ships held fast. Then, much to the pirates' consternation, the *Henry* slowly began to right itself.

The pirates began to fear the *Royal James* would not free itself in time to afford escape. The crew began pleading with Bonnet to surrender, preferring to take their chances with a court rather than cannon shot. Bonnet would have none of it. He threatened to shoot anyone who refused to fight. While they argued, Rhett's crew quickly repaired the *Henry*'s damaged rigging and prepared the sails. As the *Royal James* lay idle, the *Henry* closed the distance and prepared for boarding. Bonnet ordered the *Royal James*'s powder magazine blown. However, before anyone could act, the crew convinced Bonnet to surrender.

The six-hour Battle of Cape Fear River was costly. The *Sea Nymph* suffered two dead and four wounded. The *Henry* suffered ten killed and

Stede Bonnet being brought before Colonel Rhett after the terrible Battle of Cape Fear. *Colonel Rhett and the Pirate,* by Howard Pyle (1853–1911). *Courtesy of Wikimedia Commons.*

fourteen wounded (some of whom later died). The *Royal James* saw seven dead and five wounded (two of whom later died). The surviving pirates were taken aboard the *Henry*, and it was only then that Rhett discovered he had been engaged in battle with Bonnet and not Vane. On October 3, the *Henry* and the *Sea Nymph*, with captives in hand, limped into Charleston Harbor.

Since Bonnet was of noble birth, he could not be imprisoned with common criminals. He was therefore placed under house arrest at the town marshal's residence, under the watchful eyes of two guards. He was soon joined by two fellow crewmen, David Herriott and Ignatius Pell, who agreed to turn king's evidence and so were separated from the rest of the crew for their own safety. As a nobleman, Bonnet had the support of many in the city. There was actual resistance to Bonnet being put on trial, which resulted in some civil unrest. Charleston officials responded swiftly, passing an act that allowed for speedy trial of captured pirates. But on October 25, just days before the trial was to commence, Bonnet and Herriott escaped. Pell decided to take his chance at trial and remained behind.

The escape was well planned. A small sailboat was waiting, and Bonnet and Herriott, along with two other men who wished to become pirates, set sail. Contrary winds prevented the pirates from getting far, and they ultimately beached their boat on Sullivan's Island, just a few miles from Charleston. Once again, Colonel Rhett was summoned. A tip led the colonel and his men to Sullivan's Island. After a thorough search, they came upon the pirates' camp. Not wishing to take any chances, Rhett's men opened fire, killing Herriott and seriously injuring the other two men. Bonnet surrendered. During his absence, twenty-nine members of his crew had been found guilty of piracy and were hanged on November 8. Two days later, Bonnet was brought to trial.

Virginia's governor, Alexander Spotswood, wanted to end Blackbeard's reign. Witnesses testified that Blackbeard had reneged on the king's pardon, though he continued to take residence in Bath. Spotswood decided to send in both naval and land forces on a surprise raid of Bath. While Spotswood was planning the attack, Blackbeard was on Ocracoke Island, entertaining fellow pirates the likes of Charles Vane, "Calico Jack" Rackham and Robert Deal. They spent a week partying together around roaring bonfires. Vane tried to convince Blackbeard to join him in a grand attack on Nassau, but Blackbeard had other plans. He wanted to fortify Ocracoke and turn it into his own pirate haven. In the midst of their festivities, their onetime comrade, Stede Bonnet, was brought to trial and found guilty of piracy on November 12.

Following the departure of the land forces, two ships with a force of sixty men departed Norfolk on November 17. Lieutenant Robert Maynard was in command and made the larger ship, *Jane*, his flagship and assigned a Mr. Hyde to command the smaller *Ranger*. Off the coast of North Carolina, Maynard stopped several vessels and discovered Blackbeard was presently on Ocracoke. On the evening of November 21, Maynard dropped anchor outside Ocracoke Inlet. He needed good light in order to navigate the treacherous shoals and unfamiliar channels of the inlet so planned for battle at dawn.

Blackbeard, who had dispatched part of his crew to Bath, had left no watch so was unaware of Maynard's presence. However, thanks to a letter from Tobias Knight, he was warned he was being pursued and therefore expected an attack. Rather than flee, Blackbeard chose to stay and defend his future pirate fortress. While Maynard's men were busy preparing for battle, Blackbeard and his crew caroused late into the evening.

At first light, Maynard ordered small boats to take soundings and to help lead the *Jane* and *Ranger* through the shoals and into the bay. The pirates became aware of Maynard's presence, and when the small boats were within range, they fired on the smaller vessels. With surprise no longer an option, the *Jane* and *Ranger* each unfurled their Union Jacks and entered the channel, making way for the *Adventure*. Blackbeard cut his anchor line, hoisted his sails and positioned his enemy on his starboard side. As the *Jane* and *Ranger* closed, the *Adventure* made way for a narrow channel that ran along the shoreline, putting himself between the island and his enemy. Sporadic musket fire erupted from all three ships.

Maynard gave chase, but being unfamiliar with the channel's location, he ran his two ships aground. Blackbeard then ordered his eight starboard cannons fired: four at the *Ranger* and four at the *Jane*. The incredible force of the simultaneous eight-cannon broadside thrust the *Adventure* to port, grounding it on the shallow shoreline. Aboard the *Ranger*, Mr. Hyde was killed, and his second and third officers were dead or severely wounded. The damage to the *Ranger* was so extensive that it was immediately knocked out of action. A third of the *Jane*'s crew was killed or wounded. However, with the *Ranger* adrift, Maynard realized it was up to the *Jane* to carry out the remainder of the attack.

With all three ships grounded, it became a race against time between Maynard and Blackbeard to see who could float first. Maynard was especially in dire straits, as he lacked cannon and was limited to muzzle fire. He ordered his men to jettison ballast and water barrels and to work the heavy oars to quickly free themselves before Blackbeard unleashed another broadside. The *Jane* floated first, and Maynard ordered the bulk of his surviving crew below deck, both out of fear that another cannon blast would decimate his crew and to try and trick the aggressive pirate into believing Maynard had few men left with which to fight.

As the *Jane* closed in, the pirates used grappling hooks to pull the two ships together. They lobbed homemade grenades (bottles filled with black powder, small shot and bits of scrap iron) onto the *Jane*'s deck. Since the crew was hiding in the hold, the grenades had very little effect except to cover *Jane*'s deck in a thick smoke. Blackbeard, seeing only a couple men moving about the enemy ship, took the bait and ordered his crew over the gunwales. The *Jane*'s deck was slick with blood and human flesh from the broadside, and the dead lay where they fell. As the pirates poured across the gunwale, Maynard called for his men to attack. His crew sprang out of the hold, their cutlasses slashing and pistols firing.

Even with the injuries to Maynard's crew, they still outnumbered the pirates. As the men fell into close hand-to-hand combat, Blackbeard fired several of his pistols and swung his cutlass in giant, arching sweeps, slashing at anyone in his path. And then, in a truly epic moment, Maynard and Blackbeard came face to face. They each took aim with their flintlocks and fired. Blackbeard's shot went wide, while Maynard's exploded into the pirate's torso. Seemingly unaffected, the enraged Blackbeard lunged forward, his cutlass raised high to deliver a deathblow. Maynard, using both hands, lifted

The final bloody battle between Blackbeard and Lieutenant Maynard aboard the decks of the *Jane*. *Capture of the Pirate, Blackbeard, 1718*, by Jean Leon Gerome Ferris. *Courtesy of Wikimedia Commons.*

his sword above his head to ward off the strike. Blackbeard's cutlass came crashing down with such force that it snapped the lieutenant's sword at the hilt. Maynard stumbled back, hurling the useless handle at Blackbeard to try and slow the maniacal pirate.

Seeing he had the advantage, Blackbeard lifted his cutlass to deliver a second deathblow. While Maynard attempted to draw another pistol, one of his crew, seeing the lieutenant's predicament, stepped behind the pirate and slashed him across the neck. Blood shot from the pirate's throat, and his cutlass's downward blow was sent slightly askew, cutting into Maynard's knuckles but sparing his life. Maynard's crew, who had been reluctant to directly engage the crazed Blackbeard, saw the pirate weakening and descended on him from all sides with muzzles, cutlasses and knives. Blackbeard continued swinging his cutlass and shouting defiantly while being shot, slashed and stabbed. While in the process of withdrawing and cocking another pistol, he collapsed dead. In the end, it took five pistol shots and twenty severe cutlass and knife wounds to bring down the mighty Blackbeard.

When the pirates saw their captain fall, some jumped overboard and swam to shore. The rest dropped their weapons and pleaded mercy. The *Jane*'s crew quickly boarded the *Adventure*, narrowly averting disaster as they found Caesar, one of Blackbeard's most loyal crewmen, trying to set fire to the powder room (as Blackbeard had ordered him to do should he be captured or killed) intending to blow both vessels out of the water. Of Maynard's original crew, eleven were dead and twenty-four were wounded. Ten pirates, including Blackbeard, had died, with the remainder injured. The battle over, Maynard severed Blackbeard's head and hung it from the bowsprit of the *Jane* as both a trophy and proof that the legendary pirate was dead. Blackbeard's body was unceremoniously tossed overboard.

Eighteen days later, on December 10, Stede "the Gentleman Pirate" Bonnet was hanged, bringing about a dramatic end to the Golden Age of Piracy.

# 6

# CANNONS AND CHARACTERS

To state that someone is nothing more than a footnote in history is meant to be derogatory. There is a presumption that history is somehow reserved for only a select few. But in history, as in life, greatness often reveals itself in small acts of kindness, meager glimpses of courage and simple gestures of good will. In Wilmington, there are thousands of incredible stories worthy of being footnotes in history. Here are a few worth expanding on.

## KING WAT-COOSA

Around fifteen thousand years ago, the first humans settled along the banks of the Cape Fear River in the vicinity of present-day Wilmington. Acidic, sandy soil destroyed most of the archaeological evidence of these early settlers, while European warfare and disease decimated the population before their history could be recorded. The name by which these American Indians described themselves is unknown. Today, they are simply known as the Cape Fear Indians. No one can say for certain whether they were an Algonquian-, Siouan- or Iroquois-speaking tribe; however, they were distant blood relations of the Plains Sioux, though culturally they were closer to the Waccamaws. By the time Europeans permanently settled the area, the few Cape Fear Indian survivors had already fled the area.

After many failed attempts by Europeans to colonize the Cape Fear region, William Hilton arrived in 1662, exploring the shores of the river in detail as

Though little is known of the Cape Fear Indians, it's believed they lived a very similar lifestyle to the Croatan Indians, as depicted by John White in 1585. *Courtesy of Wikimedia Commons.*

an advance scout for a possible settlement party from Barbados. Hilton made note of the countryside teeming with wildlife, including large, colorful flocks of Carolina parakeets, which have since been hunted to extinction. The land was arable, and massive old-growth trees were plentiful. He encountered the Cape Fear Indians, and though there was some conflict, overall Hilton described the indigenous population favorably. The Indians fished from canoes, hunted with bows, had fields of corn, collected acorns and raised cattle and swine (left from earlier expeditions). They lived in huts in small communities and used pottery and weaved baskets.

On Big Island, Hilton met with Indian leaders, including King Wat-Coosa. Through hand gestures and sign language, Hilton communicated to King Wat-Coosa his desire to purchase the land on either side of the river. The king must have thought Hilton to be a foolish man, because no one can really "own" the land. However, perhaps simply to amuse the Europeans, the king agreed to sell Captain Hilton the "land" and "water" of the Cape Fear. The transaction was consummated with King Wat-Coosa giving Captain Hilton a gift of his two daughters.

Captain Hilton later wrote that the two young women were tall and very handsome, though undoubtedly his wife would have held a slightly different opinion. Regardless, the king's daughters climbed into the captain's boat, intent on spending the rest of their lives with their eccentric "landowner" husband. A flustered Captain Hilton finally offered King Wat-Coosa and the women a gift of a hatchet and beads, promising to return in four days for the two daughters. The two women exited the boat, and Hilton and his men departed.

Legend says that for the rest of their lives the two daughters would oftentimes stand on the bank of the river looking southward, awaiting the return of Captain Hilton. Hilton's settlement party did arrive in 1664, minus the captain, who perhaps abstained from taking part in the colonization at the urging of his wife.

# Ecce Homo

From 1739 to 1748, England and Spain were engaged in the War of Jenkins' Ear, which eventually grew into the War of Austrian Succession. Both sides engaged in privateering, and it was not uncommon for Spanish ships to attack colonial ships off the coast of the Carolinas. On several occasions,

Spanish privateers lay in wait at the mouth of the Cape Fear River before attacking ocean-bound ships as they emerged from the river. On September 3, 1748, two Spanish sloops, the twenty-four-gun flagship *Fortuna* and the twenty-gun *Loretta* with a total contingent of 260 men and under the guise of the Union Jack, boldly sailed upriver for a surprise attack on Brunswick Town, a now-abandoned village south of present-day Wilmington.

On their way upriver, several dozen Spanish privateers rowed ashore. Through a coordinated attack, the ships opened fire on Brunswick Town as the land troops charged in from the southern forest, muskets blazing. The townspeople were completely taken by surprise and were unable to organize. They were forced to abandon the village to the marauders, and several citizens were taken prisoner. The Spanish took the *Nancy*, a New England sloop, as a prize and outfitted it with twenty men and two guns. For three days, the Spanish plundered the village without resistance.

On September 6, an armed contingent of townspeople and neighboring farmers organized and counterattacked. They charged the village, surprising the Spanish, who were spread throughout the town, still greedily raiding homes. This time, the Spanish were forced to flee under the cover of cannon fire from the *Fortuna* and with a loss of at least ten killed and thirty captured. Once safely aboard their ships, which were anchored just out of range of enemy muskets, the *Fortuna* began pounding the village with cannon fire.

After twenty minutes of relentless bombardment, one of the townspeople spotted flames on the forward deck of the *Fortuna*. From shore, the Spaniards could be seen trying to combat the flames, but the fire spread quickly. Suddenly, a tremendous explosion ripped the ship apart, the flames having reached the ship's magazine. Ninety men, including the captain and his entire staff, were instantly killed. The upper decks of the ship vanished, splintering apart. Only the superstructure remained, sinking into the muck of the river.

Despite the townspeople's elation over the self-destruction of the *Fortuna*, within minutes, the *Nancy* and the *Loretta* began raining cannon fire on Brunswick Town. However, with no strategic advantage to an unrelenting barrage, and after a senseless and futile attempt at a formal truce, the Spanish prepared to abandon their siege.

Late that evening, under the cover of darkness, Major John Swann and a contingent of 130 men from Wilmington made landfall just north of Brunswick Town. Fear of being mistaken for the enemy kept them from entering the village until the morning of September 7, just after the departure of the surviving Spanish ships. The *Loretta* dropped anchor off Bald Head

*Ecce Homo* or *Behold the Man*, attributed to Francisco Pacheco (1564–1654). This painting survived the Spanish Invasion of 1748 and is currently on display at St. James Episcopal Church. *Photo by John Hirchak.*

Island and quickly sent a messenger ashore to negotiate a prisoner swap with Major Swann. Major Swann readily agreed. However, since the Spanish prisoners had already departed for Wilmington, the agreed upon deadline passed with no exchange, and the Spanish weighed anchor.

The invasion proved a disaster. Well over half of the 260 privateers were either killed or taken prisoner. The vast majority of Brunswick Town's plunder was aboard the *Fortuna* and thus destroyed in the explosion. After the Spanish departed, the colonists rowed out to the *Fortuna*'s superstructure to salvage anything of value. Most, but not all, of the recovered items, including goods stolen by the privateers in earlier raids, were sold and used to partially compensate the people of Brunswick Town.

However, one item, found hanging in the captain's quarters, was given as a gift to help aid in the completion of the church in Wilmington. It is a painting from the sixteenth century that depicts Christ wearing a crown of thorns. The painting is titled *Ecce Homo* ("Behold the Man"). The gift was accepted by the Church of England in Wilmington at the corner of Third and Market Streets, which is today known as St. James Episcopal Church. The painting remains at the church on public display.

# THE SEA DEVIL

During the Civil War, the Federal blockade of the Cape Fear River was essentially an impossible task, leaving Wilmington the last major port open to the Confederacy. The two entrance points to the river were nine miles apart; treacherous to navigate due to shallow, shifting shoals; and protected by the fiery cannons of Fort Fisher and Fort Caswell. The city of Wilmington was also too far inland and upriver to bombard, leaving it virtually untouched until the end of the Civil War.

Though blockade running could be quite lucrative, it was a truly hazardous business. At least thirty wrecks litter the Wilmington shoreline, while a far greater number were captured. The average career of a blockade runner was just two round-trips. Yet despite the overwhelming odds, some captains found great success.

John Newland Maffitt was born at sea on February 22, 1819, making him a true son of Neptune. He spent a considerable amount of his childhood in the Cape Fear Valley before enlisting in the U.S. Navy at the age of thirteen. By age sixteen, he was serving as a commodore's aide aboard the USS *Constitution*, one of the greatest warships of its era. For a period of fifteen years, beginning in 1842, Maffitt commanded ships responsible for mapping the Atlantic coast shoreline, filling him with an intimate knowledge that would benefit him later in his career. In 1858, he was placed in command of the USS *Dolphin*, which was responsible for suppressing pirates and the illegal slave trade. His command was personally responsible for the capture of three slave ships and the rescue and release of approximately 850 slaves.

Maffitt was at his home in Washington when news of the battle at Fort Sumter reached the city. Despite his service, as a son of the South, he was eyed suspiciously. With his wife's recent death, his children were sent south to live with family. Unable to collect his navy back pay or to sell his Washington home, and with his loyalties torn between state and country, Maffitt resigned his post. Amid rumors of his impending arrest, he fled the city.

John Newland Maffit was also known as the Sea Devil, based on his daring escapades as a blockade runner. *Courtesy of New Hanover Public Library.*

Maffitt enlisted in the Confederate States Navy. In 1862, he was placed in command of the 191-foot, sail- and steam engine–driven cruiser CSS *Florida*. His range stretched from Halifax, Nova Scotia, to Cape Horn, South America, and all ports and islands in between. While in command of the *Florida*, he captured over forty United States merchant ships. He also successfully and repeatedly penetrated Union blockades into and out of Wilmington, Pensacola, Galveston and Mobile. Though he was often pursued by a large squadron of Federal ships, he was never captured.

In the fall of 1863, near Cárdenas, Cuba, Maffitt and the crew of *Florida* contracted yellow fever. In an extraordinary display of bravado—with only five able-bodied seamen, lacking the ability to fire its guns and in broad daylight—Maffitt led the stricken *Florida* in an audacious dash through the heavily fortified Union blockade of Mobile. Union ships unleashed a fierce fusillade of cannon fire on the *Florida*, shredding its decks and crew apart, but they were unable to stop or sink it. The *Florida* limped into Mobile Bay under the safety of Fort Morgan's guns. The damage to the *Florida* was so severe that it took more than three months to refit and repair it.

Wishing to keep Maffitt literally at bay, the Union navy bolstered its blockade force. Yet, under cover of a raging January storm, Maffitt led the *Florida* on a charge into the middle of the Union line. Six Union ships descended on the *Florida* and seemingly had it in their grasps, but the cagey John Maffitt somehow eluded capture. This embarrassment to the Union navy was followed several months later by Maffitt's daring escape from Pensacola. Despite the Union forces being forewarned of his planned departure time, and with a meager one-mile-wide port entrance guarded by seven Union ships, Maffitt slipped through the blockade.

In February 1864, Maffitt, still battling the lingering effects of yellow fever, relinquished his command of the *Florida*. After months recuperating, he returned to a new command off the coast of North Carolina, eventually taking charge of the 230-foot, 771-ton, steel-hulled sidewheeler the CSS *Owl*. Maffitt made dozens of successful blockade runs with the *Owl*, including several to Wilmington. On one run out of Wilmington, the *Owl* took nine cannon shots, wounding the captain and several crewmen, before escaping to sea. Aboard the *Owl*, Maffitt made the Confederacy's last blockade run of the war.

Though Maffitt is best remembered as one of the Civil War's most successful blockade runners, he was also responsible for the capture or sinking of over seventy enemy ships, worth an estimated $15 million. He was often referred to as the "Prince of Privateers," but in actuality, he was not a privateer. His other sobriquet, the "Sea Devil," was much more accurate and befitting.

John Newland Maffitt died on his two-hundred-acre farm along Bradley Creek in 1886.

# Philip Bassadiere

After the devastating fire of 1819, in which over three hundred homes, businesses and secondary buildings were lost, residents realized axes and buckets of water were useless in the face of an inferno. They were eager for a more modern, scientific and intelligent approach to dealing with such conflagrations. Naturally, the city's politicians took the opposite approach.

They declared that during the next great fire, they would order all the buildings in the conflagration's path to be blown up in order to create a firewall.

It was in this environment that Philip Bassadiere (pronounced fuh-LEEP bah-sod-ee-AY) arrived in Wilmington. Philip came from Pointe-à-Pitre, on the island of Guadeloupe. His manners were polished, and he spoke with a rich, tropical French accent, enunciating every syllable as though each were of the utmost importance. He dressed impeccably and would always greet people with a slight bow of the head, a lifting of his hat and the words, "Your servant, Sir." He was also the trumpeter for the Wilmington Light Horse Guards. During parades, dressed in a scarlet coat, doe-skin breeches and black-top boots, he would gallop his horse ahead of the other soldiers, stopping at each intersection and giving a mighty blow of his trumpet. Children loved him and would follow him about in great mobs.

Philip owned and operated a basement barbershop on the first block of North Front Street, in the vicinity of today's Masonic temple. Customers would enter through a basement door off a side alleyway and, after negotiating a narrow hallway, arrive at his secluded parlor. One afternoon, while business was at a lull, Philip slipped into one of his fine leather barber's chairs and stole a nap. Unbeknownst to him, a fire broke out a few doors away. Tucked away in the basement and deep in slumber, Philip didn't hear the fire bells clanging. While he slept, giant barrels of black powder were rolled into the surrounding buildings. Citizens went door to door, making sure buildings were vacant. But alas, they missed poor Philip.

As the fire raged, the fuses were lit and the citizenry ran away. An enormous explosion rocked North Front Street, sending massive chunks of mortar, brick and wood hundreds of feet into the air. And there among the detritus, clinging to his fine leather-bound barber's chair, was a screaming Philip Bassadiere. He flew like no man was meant to fly, crashing back down to earth in a pile of debris. Firemen raced to the site of his impact and quickly retrieved his badly battered body, not wanting to add insult to injury by allowing his remains to be destroyed by fire. As they dragged his limp body away, he let out a low moan.

"My God, he's alive!" one of the firemen yelled.

How anyone could have survived such an ordeal was beyond all present, but survive he did—sort of. Unfortunately, his fantastic journey through the sky rattled his brain and left him mentally and emotionally scarred. Upon recovering from his wounds, Philip turned to tipping the old Johnny Barleycorn, and within a year, he drank himself to death.

# A Purple Heart

When the USS *North Carolina* was commissioned on April 9, 1941, it was America's first new battleship since 1923. At a total cost of almost $77 million, it was perhaps the world's most awesome concentration of sea firepower. With a length of 728.8 feet and a beam of 108.3 feet, it came in at thirty-six thousand tons and was capable of a top speed of twenty-six knots. Its armament included nine 16.0-inch guns, twenty 5.0-inch guns, sixteen 1.1-inch guns (later replaced with fifteen quad 40mm antiaircraft guns) and forty-six single 20mm cannons. Its upgraded, modern 16.0-inch guns were capable of firing a 2,700-pound shell at a range of twenty-one miles (that's the equivalent of launching a Honda Accord from downtown Wilmington to Southport).

During its sea trials, the *North Carolina* received so much attention that it was dubbed the "Showboat." On the eve of the attack on Pearl Harbor, while completing its shakedown cruise in the Caribbean, its destiny was still unknown, but within six short months, its effect on the Pacific theater of operations would be felt. Its arrival in Pearl Harbor immediately boosted morale. On July 15, it departed with a task force of eleven ships to begin its telling battle career.

Its complement of 144 officers and 2,195 enlisted men knew, after sixteen months of vigorous training, that the *North Carolina* was an able ship. It took just eight minutes, on August 24, 1942, during the Battle of the Eastern Solomons, for the crew to discover it was also a lucky ship. During an attack from Japanese divebombers, torpedo bombers and fighters, the *North Carolina* was narrowly missed seven times. Its antiaircraft guns fired 841 rounds of 5.0-inch shells, 1,037 rounds of 1.1 inch ammunition, 7,425 rounds of 20mm shells and 8,641 rounds of .50-caliber bullets, shooting down between seven and fourteen enemy aircraft. The eight-minute defensive barrage was so intense that the aircraft carrier USS *Enterprise* mistook the thundering fusillade and resulting smoke as the result of a direct hit on the *North Carolina*.

Though the Japanese heavily targeted the *North Carolina*, claiming to have sunk it on six separate occasions, its defenses were nearly impenetrable. Despite having sailed over 300,000 miles, participating in every major naval offensive in the Pacific, receiving fifteen battle stars and being the most highly decorated battleship of World War II, it was struck by only one torpedo and a single aerial bomb and hit once by friendly fire. Every other torpedo, bomb and kamikaze attack was either repelled or averted. Despite a complement of 2,339 seamen, it lost only 10 crewmen in action and suffered 67 wounded.

The berthing of the USS *North Carolina* in 1961. Fergus's Ark Restaurant was docked at the foot of Princess Street, near the federal customs and courthouse. *Courtesy of New Hanover Public Library.*

On June 27, 1947, the USS *North Carolina* was decommissioned and sent to languish at a mooring at a New Jersey naval yard. In 1960, the once mighty ship was stricken from the Naval Vessel Registry. Through the "Save Our Ship" campaign, $330,000 was raised, mainly from spare change and lunch money donated by North Carolina schoolchildren, to purchase the Showboat from the U.S. Navy. In 1961, six years before the construction of the Cape Fear Bridge, which would have prevented the completion of the *North Carolina*'s final journey, a fleet of tugboats guided the majestic ship up the Cape Fear River and into historic Wilmington.

At the time, a rescued U.S. Army troopship was tied off at the end of Princess Street, near where the U.S. Coast Guard cutter *Diligence* is presently moored. The troopship was refitted as a restaurant named Fergus's Ark. As the 728-foot, thirty-six-thousand-ton battleship was being swung about, the contingent of tugboats temporarily lost control. The battleship, which is longer than the river is wide, struck Fergus's Ark, crushing the stern and causing severe enough damage to cause the closure of the restaurant. The *North Carolina* was quickly brought back under control and nestled into its final berth.

The owner of the restaurant was a good-humored man. He announced that since Fergus's Ark was wounded while in the service of its country, it deserved a medal. With great fanfare, he had a fifteen-foot-tall Purple Heart painted on the side of his restaurant.

# BRANDON LEE

Brandon Bruce Lee was only eight years old when his father, the legendary martial arts film actor Bruce Lee, died at the age of thirty-two while filming the movie *Game of Death*. Brandon, like his father, was a gifted martial artist who was drawn to the craft of acting. His first role was in *Kung Fu: The Movie*, which aired on Brandon's twenty-first birthday. Through great passion, training and a rigorous work ethic, Brandon advanced through the corridors of Hollywood. In 1993, he landed the coveted lead role of Eric Draven in a film that was expected to launch him to stardom: *The Crow*.

At its most basic level, *The Crow*, which was based on a popular underground comic book, is about a murdered rock star who comes back from the dead to avenge his murder and that of his fiancée. The gothic thriller was considerably violent and had some martial arts fighting, but for the most part, Brandon's acting ability would be relied on to capture Draven's essence.

Filming began on February 1, 1993, at what is now known as Screen Gems Studios in Wilmington (at the time the largest film studio outside Los Angeles). The shooting schedule was to last sixty-seven days, with a wrap date of April 8. Nine days later, on April 17, Brandon and his real-life fiancée, Eliza Hutton, were to be married in Ensenada, Mexico.

During filming, there was a lot of buzz about the movie regarding the incredible gothic sets, the great range of characters and Brandon's obvious ability to carry the lead. On March 30, with the wrap date just over a week away, the crew was preparing to shoot its final all-night scene and the final scene involving guns. Before departing for the studio, Brandon called his mother to discuss final arrangements for his and Eliza's upcoming wedding. During their conversation, Brandon told his mother how pleased he was with the quality of the film and how confident he was that it would be well received. A short while later, he walked onto soundstage number four.

The scene they were preparing to shoot actually takes place at the start of the movie. In the scene, Brandon's character, Eric Draven, enters his apartment carrying a bag of groceries. As Draven steps into the apartment, he discovers a gang of drug dealers beating up his onscreen fiancée. One of the drug dealers, Funboy, turns and shoots Draven with a .44, while another character, T-Bird, shouts insults at the rock star's crumpled body. Several cameras were used to try to capture the extremely chaotic and complicated scene in a single take.

Several real-time effects were used to help sell the scene. The .44 was loaded with blank rounds packed with a stronger than normal gunpowder. When the trigger was pulled, not only would it sound as loud as a real gunshot, but also the more powerful powder would produce a convincing muzzle flash. In addition, Brandon was fitted with two squibs and a blood bag. When the .44 was fired, Brandon would squeeze a device concealed in his hand that would trigger the squibs, exploding out the bag and his shirt, just as though a bullet had been shot through them, and rupture the blood bag, causing a convincing amount of blood to flow out of the supposed bullet wound, soaking his shirt and pooling on the floor.

The full scene, without real-time effects, was rehearsed several times. When everyone felt comfortable and ready, film began to roll, and the director called, "Action!" Immediately, it was clear the scene was not unfolding as planned. Funboy stumbled as he turned to fire the .44, and though Brandon triggered the squibs and blood bag, he did not fall the same way he had just rehearsed. Everyone assumed Brandon was simply improvising, as he had done repeatedly throughout filming. Though T-Bird began shouting insults at Draven, Brandon wasn't crawling across the floor like he was supposed to. One crew member thought he saw Brandon indicate to "cut filming" when he first fell back against the door. Another crew member thought he heard Brandon moan and thought he was trying to lift his hand. Despite these irregularities, nearly a minute would pass before the director yelled, "Cut!"

Immediately, Jeff Imada, a stuntman and close friend of Brandon's, raced over, thinking his friend had hit his head on the door when he fell backward, knocking himself unconscious. Imada checked the back of Brandon's head, but there was no blood or lump. With each passing second of Brandon being completely non-responsive, Imada became more and more concerned. Someone quickly realized that the amount of blood pooling on the floor was more than the blood bag could hold. Imada lifted Lee's shirt for a closer examination and found a one-inch slit next to Brandon's navel.

An investigation later determined what had happened. In the preceding scene, dummy bullets were placed in the gun's cylinder. Typically, a dummy bullet is a simple prop, an actual fake bullet. But in this case, real bullets were used. The bullets were emptied of their powder, reinserted in their casing,

Brandon Bruce Lee's final resting place. *Courtesy of Wikimedia Commons.*

and then loaded into the .44's cylinders. Overlooked was the fact that though the powder was emptied, the live percussion primer remained. At some point, someone pulled the trigger of the .44, and the primer ignited with just enough force to push the bullet into the barrel where it became lodged in a condition known as "squib load." When the dummy bullets were later removed and the blank rounds inserted into the cylinders, no one realized an actual bullet was lodged in the barrel. So when the .44 was fired at Brandon, the blast from the powerful blank powder pushed the lodged dummy bullet out of the gun with a force equal to that of a live round.

Brandon was rushed to the New Hanover County Regional Medical Center, where he underwent six hours of emergency surgery and received sixty-one pints of blood. Eliza Hutton arrived at the hospital at noon. Brandon Bruce Lee was pronounced dead at 1:04 p.m.

The film that recorded Brandon being shot was destroyed without ever being developed. With encouragement from Brandon's mother and fiancée, the final scenes were shot using a double, and the film was released in 1994. Indeed, Brandon Lee's performance was critically acclaimed, and had he survived, he would have likely become the next great action/adventure star.

Brandon Bruce Lee was twenty-eight years old. He is buried beside his father in Lake View Cemetery in Washington State.

# 7

# ABRAHAM GALLOWAY

*To be heroic does not have to mean possessing the ability to stand against the evils of the world, either well or successfully, but just that one is willing to stand.*
—*Mike Alsford*

*The world is a dangerous place, not because of those who do bad things, but because of those who look on and do nothing.*
—*Albert Einstein*

Abraham Galloway was born the son of John Wesley Galloway, a white aristocrat, and Hester Hankins, a black slave. According to the antebellum laws of North Carolina, and despite his father's station, Abraham was considered mere human chattel—a slave and the rightful property of his mother's owner, Milton Hankins.

Milton Hankins worked for the Wilmington & Manchester Railroad. Shortly after Abraham's birth, Hankins settled in a home in the 800 block of North Fourth Street with his wife, Abraham and two female slaves (one of whom was Hester Hankins). At the time, Wilmington was the largest and most prosperous city in North Carolina, roughly the size and population of Atlanta. An international demand for cotton and naval stores helped to fuel Wilmington's growth. As the port and railroad expanded, infrastructure needs kept the city in a near-constant building boom. By his eleventh birthday, Galloway had begun apprenticing as a brick mason. He spent the remainder of his childhood and early adult years learning all there was to know about his craft, from forming and firing bricks to laying them.

After his apprenticeship, and upon becoming a master brick mason, Hankins allowed Galloway to seek his own masonry jobs, provided he pay $180 annually into the Hankins household (the equivalent of around $35,000 today). This arrangement was common between skilled-labor slaves and their owners. For Hankins, who had inherited his slaves at a young age and, as a train mechanic, was a man of little means, he was afforded some financial security. For Galloway, this meant a small level of freedom rarely provided to slaves and allowed him the opportunity, through hard work over a significant period of time, to save his money and, perhaps, one day purchase his and his mother's freedom.

Despite decades of growing abolitionist sentiment in the Northeast, the United States government seemed either indifferent toward or incapable of ending slavery. Time and again, elected officials would collapse under pressure from the slave-owning states. Still, for those in bondage, there was always a glimmer of hope that the government would one day recognize the hypocrisy of being born under the phrase "all men are created equal" while at the same time supporting the institution of bondage. Then, on March 6, 1857, the Supreme Court announced its ruling on what is now known as the Dred Scott decision. Through a complete misinterpretation of the Constitution, and in what is undoubtedly the worst decision ever handed down by the Supreme Court, the court ruled that the United States government had no power to regulate slavery and that no person of African descent, whether free or slave, could ever be a U.S. citizen. To slaves and freemen alike, the message was clear: the United States government had officially abandoned them.

When news of the Dred Scott decision reached Wilmington, Galloway confided to one of his closest friends and a fellow slave, Richard Eden, that he was prepared to fight and, if necessary, die to gain his freedom. Eden concurred. The two men agreed to act cautiously but quickly. Due to Milton Hankins's constant financial struggles and Galloway's increased value as a master mason, Abraham feared he would soon be sold and might end up in Mississippi or Louisiana—two states that were rumored to be notorious in their mistreatment of slaves and from which there was no chance of escape. Eden's worry was that he was nearing a punishment of thirty-nine lashes for the crime of marrying a free woman, which was illegal in North Carolina.

By June, the two men had cautiously made arrangements with a sympathetic sea captain to smuggle them north to freedom. To protect their savior, neither

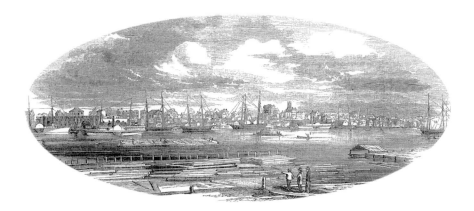

A view of Wilmington's harbor in 1853 as seen from Eagles Island. Abraham Galloway and countless other slaves helped build the port's extensive infrastructure. *Courtesy of New Hanover County Public Library.*

Galloway nor Eden ever disclosed the captain's name or how they managed to get aboard his schooner. But once aboard, they hid in the cargo hold, their freedom far from certain. At any point, they could be discovered by a crewman more than willing to turn in the runaway slaves for a sizable bounty. To their good fortune (likely due to a timely bribe from the ship's captain), the runaways were spared the typical "fogging" that was required of any ship before weighing anchor on a journey to a Northern port. Fogging was done by closing all the ship's holds and placing smoldering pots of turpentine dregs in the lower decks. Like tear gas, the smoke would burn the eyes, throat and lungs, and for stowaway slaves who refused to surrender, it was lethal. Despite its not being fogged, the ship's hold was filled with barrels of tar, rosin and turpentine, and the two men suffered greatly from the toxic fumes during their seemingly endless voyage. They arrived in Philadelphia near death.

## A FUGITIVE SLAVE

Galloway and Eden were put in contact with a local vigilance committee, and, with barely time to recover from their harrowing journey, sent north to Canada West, the present-day province of Ontario—away from the hands of slave hunters. Galloway briefly worked as a brick mason, but within weeks, he became active in the greater effort to free his people from bondage. Canada

West had a large fugitive slave and freedman population, and it took little effort for Galloway to find people of similar convictions. Though Galloway understood that the Fugitive Slave Act of 1850 meant that if he were ever captured, he would be either hanged or re-enslaved, he began to venture back into the United States to deliver powerful antislavery speeches and to work with the abolitionist movement.

Galloway's initial travels introduced him to two movements that would forever influence his life. First and foremost, he became involved with a militant black abolitionist group that not only preached for an end to slavery, but was also prepared to fight for it. He actively smuggled runaway slaves over the Kentucky-Ohio border and learned the art of self-defense and deception in order to avoid capture. The second movement, at some levels indistinguishable from the first, was the antislavery/abolitionist movement coming out of Boston. It was there that he was introduced to, and soon befriended, two prominent leaders: William Lloyd Garrison, one of America's most influential abolitionists, and George L. Stearns, perhaps best known for supplying weaponry to John Brown during Brown's brutal guerrilla war against the forces of slavery in the Kansas Territory. Stearns later went on to help form the Fifty-fourth Regiment, as was depicted in the movie *Glory*.

During one of his stays in Boston, Abraham was party to near-riots between white mobs and black abolitionist leaders such as Frederick Douglass. As the riots unfolded, Abraham came to realize that though there were white abolitionists willing to fight to end slavery, the public at large was not prepared to give their lives for such a proposition. He concluded that the only way for the slave to free himself of his oppressor was by taking up arms against him. So, in January 1861, Abraham set sail for Haiti, in part to help establish a black exile community and in part to help plan and participate in an armed invasion of the Southern states. George Stearns was helping arm Haitian forces, and though Abraham worked diligently to try to realize Stearns's dream, after several months, the plan fell apart. Abraham returned to the States, arriving in New York days before the Battle of Fort Sumter and the start of the American Civil War.

## THE UNION SPY

At the strong recommendation of Stearns, Union leaders recruited Galloway as a spy. Galloway's skills, desire and near-fearlessness immediately proved invaluable to the Union cause. For the duration of the war, Galloway made extensive excursions behind enemy lines into practically every Confederate state. He recruited slaves throughout the South to aid him in intelligence gathering, reconnaissance and, ultimately, combat. His efforts helped lead Union forces to many military victories, including the taking of key North Carolina cities along the northeast coast. By the spring of 1862, thanks in no small part to his efforts, Cape Hatteras, Roanoke Island, Plymouth, Washington, Beaufort and New Bern had fallen under Union control. The Union would not relinquish this foothold for the remainder of the war.

One of Galloway's first acts after the fall of New Bern was to set up a means whereby coastal North Carolina slaves could escape to Union-held territory. Then, Galloway set sail with Union forces to New Orleans, where they hoped to seize control of the mouth of the Mississippi River. Again, Galloway infiltrated Confederate strongholds, gathered invaluable intelligence and recruited slaves to aid in the Union army's invasion. On May 1, 1862, New Orleans fell and, like New Bern, would remain in Union hands for the rest of the war. However, New Orleans was only part of Galloway's mission. Ultimately, Union forces needed to take Vicksburg, Mississippi, two hundred miles upriver from New Orleans. If Vicksburg fell, the Confederacy would be divided, and the Union would control the entire length of the Mississippi River.

Though Union troops would fail to take Vicksburg in 1862, two events transpired that helped cement Galloway's belief that the only way for slaves to gain and secure their freedom was by personally taking up arms against their oppressors in both the North and South. The first event was his encounter with slaves as an advance scout for the Union army. In Louisiana and Mississippi, where the slave population far outnumbered the white population, an extreme level of brutality was used to keep the slaves under minority control. Galloway was likely familiar with Solomon Northrup's memoir *Twelve Years a Slave*; however, he was ill prepared for the level of carnage he came upon. Nearly every black man, woman and child he encountered bore the ghastly scars of countless beatings and whippings. Yet these people were not broken, and they were prepared to fight. Galloway realized that, if given the means, no man could fight an oppressor more fiercely than the oppressed.

The second event was the betrayal and abandonment of his fellow slaves by the very Union forces for which they were putting their lives at risk. Union forces had recruited the help of over one thousand slaves to dig a river bypass of Vicksburg. These slaves were promised their freedom and the Union

This 1871 drawing of Abraham Galloway was copied from what had long been considered the only known photograph of Galloway. The original photo was thought to be lost shortly thereafter. *Courtesy of New Hanover County Public Library.*

army's protection for their service. But when the task proved impossible, Union troops withdrew and abandoned the slaves and the black freemen, including Galloway, two hundred miles behind enemy lines. Galloway knew he could never fully trust the Union army again.

Recaptured slaves knew they would receive no mercy. All were destined for bone-breaking beatings and would face fifty to one hundred lashes. Yet no beating or whipping could compare to the terrible fate of a captured black Union spy. Galloway knew if his true identity were discovered, he would face certain death. His only hope for survival was to convince his captors he was a slave who had been seized by Union forces and made to dig the attempted bypass of Vicksburg. Even then, the prospect of survival in the Deep South was grim. Abraham Galloway must have understood he would likely never again walk this earth as a free man.

Upon hearing of his abandonment, Galloway's friends in the North feared the worst. The punishment for a captured Union spy was death. As months passed and the war continued to rage on, his fate remained a mystery. Then, five months after his capture, a badly beaten, half-starved Abraham Galloway stumbled back into New Bern. The details of his ordeal and escape are a mystery, as Galloway rarely spoke of his own exploits. However, upon his recovery, he began wearing a pistol in his belt at all times. He also became more politically involved and was now recognized by the black community at large as one of the foremost representatives of freed slaves.

## THE AFRICAN BRIGADE

By May 1863, things were not going well for the Union. While Robert E. Lee handed the Confederacy another decisive victory at the Battle of Chancellorsville, this time against a force twice his size, Ulysses S. Grant was bogged down in Vicksburg, in a new attempt by Union forces to seize control of the Mississippi River. Desertion and disease were decimating Union forces, and recruitment was down. Congress was forced to initiate a draft, leading to riots in many Northern cities. It was then, at perhaps the Union's bleakest hour, that President Lincoln turned to the freed slaves of the South.

Edward Kinsley arrived in New Bern with travel papers signed by President Lincoln and Secretary of War Edwin Stanton to determine if former slaves were prepared to fight for their enduring freedom. Reports of New Bern's thousand-man-strong fugitive slave militia seemed to indicate these men were indeed ready to fight. Yet weeks passed, and Kinsley barely was able to recruit a single man. Then one evening, Kinsley was summoned to an intermediary's home, where he was blindfolded and led up to the attic. When his blindfold was removed, Kinsley stood before an attic full of black men, though one stood before all others and was clearly the leader. It was Abraham Galloway, with pistol in hand. Galloway got right to the point, telling Kinsley he had little trust in Lincoln. True, the president had issued the Emancipation Proclamation a few months earlier; however, thus far, full rights of citizenship had not been granted. Galloway also made it clear he was tired of Union troops treating freedmen as though they were still nothing more than slaves. If Lincoln wanted freedmen recruits, Galloway would deliver regiments' worth. But first, he would need to receive certain assurances.

Galloway insisted that black recruits be paid the same as white soldiers and that housing be provided for their families and schooling for their children. And, of utmost importance, he demanded that Kinsley promise that black soldiers taken prisoner by the Confederacy would be treated fairly and not hanged as traitors. Though this was something Kinsley could never guarantee—for Jefferson Davis had already signed an order stating that all blacks captured fighting for the Union, as well as white officers leading those troops, would be hanged—Kinsley promised his best to do so. When negotiations concluded, Galloway held a pistol to Kinsley's head and made him swear an oath to uphold their agreement and deliver their conditions to the president. Kinsley readily took this oath.

Galloway immediately disappeared behind enemy lines and returned a week later with a large group of newly runaway slaves. During his absence, Kinsley spoke with the Union leaders occupying New Bern and got them to agree to support all that Kinsley had promised Galloway. The day after word of this agreement reached Galloway, hundreds of ex-slaves began arriving at the recruitment office. Within days, 600 new recruits, strong from their backbreaking work as slaves, were enlisted. The African Brigade, made up exclusively of former slaves, was formed. These men were the first to become Union soldiers in and around New Bern. Over 5,000 others would follow. As word of the successful recruitment, superior conditioning and unfaltering resolve of these new recruits spread, more and more regiments formed. By war's end, over 180,000 blacks would serve in the Union army—the majority of them former slaves.

## Life Beyond Warfare

Galloway worked tirelessly, splitting his time between the North, where he solicited funds to support black troops and their families, and the South, where he continued to slip across enemy lines, freeing slaves, driving up recruitment and gathering intelligence. It was during this period that he began speaking out for full and equal rights for all people of African descent, specifically the right to vote. Yet in the midst of all he was working to accomplish, there was one bit of unfinished business that weighed heavily on him.

In the autumn of 1863, Wilmington, eighty miles south of New Bern, was a Confederate stronghold. Wilmington was the last major port open to the Confederacy and was one of the most heavily fortified cities in the South. Without the blockade runners delivering invaluable supplies up the Cape Fear River, Lee's troops in Richmond would have starved, and the Confederacy would have been forced to surrender. In one of his last acts as a Union spy, Galloway, with great personal risk, slipped behind enemy lines and back into Wilmington, a city where he was well known and recognizable. His stay was brief, but when he returned to New Bern, he had but a single runaway slave by his side. Gently, holding her by the arm, he guided his mother across the Union line and helped her take her first step as a free woman.

On December 29, Abraham Galloway married Martha Ann Dixon. As his political influence grew, he began giving speeches to larger and larger gatherings, sometimes in excess of one thousand people. Though the details of his adventures were not well documented, it was well known he had served his country admirably as a Union spy. By the spring of 1864, he was considered one of the most promising and respected leaders from the South. Though at the time, many black leaders were reluctant to antagonize the white Northerner on whom much of their freedom relied, Galloway forcefully argued for equal rights for all men, including the right to vote, and vowed to free not just the black slaves of the South but also the poor white man, who was often just as much of a victim as the slave. Galloway was becoming a true political force.

## A Political Calling

On April 29, 1864, Galloway, the leader of a delegation of Southern black men, met with President Abraham Lincoln. Though the war had been raging for just over three years, this was the first time the president had met with black leaders from the South. Lincoln greeted the men at the front door of the White House and led them inside. For many of these men, it was the first time in their lives that they had been permitted to enter the front door of a white man's home. This simple act of respect—of human decency—left an indelible impression on the group. Galloway and his delegation chronicled for the president declining Northern enlistments and how more and more men of African descent were carrying the load of battle. Hundreds of thousands of slaves were fighting and dying for their country. In return for their sacrifice, they urged the president to fight for their right to vote. Galloway reminded President Lincoln that for almost sixty years after the signing of the Declaration of Independence, North Carolina allowed freed blacks to vote. Through suffrage, Galloway reasoned, all other rights would flow. The president listened courteously but was noncommittal.

In October 1864, Galloway was elected a delegate of the National Convention of Colored Men of the United States. As president of the convention, Frederick Douglass handpicked Galloway, with whom he was already familiar and much impressed, to serve as one of four men on the executive committee. Galloway worked tirelessly, and in return, he was offered a greater national spotlight. He was quickly recognized as a powerhouse of ideas and action. Galloway found that many of the attendees at the convention were from the North and had never suffered at the hand of a slave owner. They were overly cautious in their approach and didn't want to press Washington or the general public too hard when it came to their civil rights. However, Galloway fervently argued that not only should they expect all the equal protections afforded all men by the Constitution, but also that, if denied these rights, they should be prepared to do whatever necessary to achieve them. He also argued that Northern Republicans needed to start speaking out and supporting the newly freed slaves, for the Southern white man would continue to suppress the black populations, even after losing a war over the very same issue.

## The Return Home

On February 22, 1865, Wilmington fell. Within six weeks, the Confederacy surrendered. Shortly thereafter, Galloway; his wife, Martha Ann; and his mother, Hester Hankins, returned to Wilmington, settling again in the 800 block of North Fourth Street. Galloway quickly went to work to help create a public education system for newly freed slaves. Though he was illiterate, he knew the path to power would be strengthened through an educated populace. He also helped to create a new black fire brigade and other important institutions and infrastructure necessary to the success of these recently freed people.

After the war, as Galloway predicted, the former slaveholders entrenched themselves in power. They still controlled nearly the entire economy of the South, including jobs and wages, so they were able to keep former slaves in a position of need. They also kept freed blacks in a constant state of

The Fall of Wilmington, 1865. As Confederate prisoners were being led out of Wilmington, Galloway and his family returned, moving into a house across the street from where he was once held in bondage. *Courtesy of New Hanover Public Library.*

fear through a calculated campaign of terror and violence. Union troop leaders proved either unwilling or unable to help freedmen and even failed to protect or defend their own black troops. Many Northern Republicans, exhausted from years of war, abandoned the former slaves in the belief that their victory in the war had succeeded in keeping the Union intact and was thus the finale of the long struggle. Yet Galloway tirelessly continued to fight for even the most basic of American rights.

Finally, almost two years after the war's end, the United States Congress passed the Reconstruction Act of 1867. The act required the Rebel states, including North Carolina, to create a new constitution allowing for black suffrage before being readmitted to the Union. In addition, all antebellum officeholders were banned from holding public office again. In July 1867, Galloway gave a sixty-minute speech inside Thalian Hall, urging blacks to join the Republican Party. He argued that the only path to political power was through a unified Republican Party that represented both Northern and Southern interests. Though white supremacy groups threatened violence to keep blacks from voting, Galloway and other black leaders helped organize and arm groups of men to protect and defend local polling stations. Galloway was one of three delegates elected to represent New Hanover County at the North Carolina Constitutional Congress.

The Constitutional Convention ran from January through March 1868. Though white conservatives were a minority at the convention, they were the most vocal and extreme. These were men who did not hesitate to beat a black man, woman or child for entering a white establishment through the front door or for failing to step off a sidewalk when a white person approached. Galloway would have none of it. During the convention, when Southern Democrats, white supremacists and the former slaveholders demanded deference from Abraham, he stood before them and reminded them they were talking not only to family, since his father was white, but to an aristocrat as well. Though he could be quick tempered and at times defensive, he was also able to quickly disarm his opponents through wit and humor. Regardless of his approach, he refused to bow to any man.

Despite the loud cries of the conservative class, a new constitution was passed, guaranteeing the right to vote to all men while eliminating property ownership and religious qualifications. Laws were also changed to allow for a public education system and to strengthen women's rights. Galloway returned home mostly triumphant to find out he had been nominated to run for the state senate. He celebrated with the baptism of his first son, John Galloway.

Abraham knew white conservatives were not going to casually allow blacks to either run for office or vote. While campaigning, he survived several assassination attempts, including nearly being knifed to death, shot and hanged. When laws were passed to make it a crime for a black man to own a gun, Abraham openly and defiantly wore his pistol at his side, daring any man to take it from him. As the election grew near, white supremacists again tried to keep blacks from voting; however, Galloway's black militia helped to keep all the polling stations open and safe. Abraham Galloway was one of three black senators elected to the North Carolina state legislature.

# THE SENATOR

During his first term in office, Galloway had a huge impact on the state senate. His enthusiasm and hard work resulted in many key leadership posts. Though he fought hard for freedmen's rights, he was also, in many ways, a visionary and ahead of his time. Though Susan B. Anthony had long fought for equal rights for all men and women, regardless of color, few men were as vocal as Abraham Galloway. Having seen firsthand the deplorable conditions and treatment of black women at the hands of both black and white men, he introduced and fought hard to have bills passed that allowed women the right to vote and to hold office. He also fought to give women the right to own property and to make it a crime to beat a woman. Unfortunately, most of the women's rights he fought for were still decades—and in some cases, a century—away.

By August 1870, the political landscape was rapidly changing. Divisions in the Republican Party, especially between Northern and Southern as well as black and white interests, were causing disunity. Meanwhile, Southern Democrats were becoming more unified. White supremacist groups like the Ku Klux Klan and the Regulators were in the process of a reign of terror that scared many black men away from the polls. Despite the rising anti-Republican, anti-freedman attitude, Galloway was reelected to a second term and vowed to continue in his efforts to secure the basic freedoms he felt were guaranteed to all Americans.

More and more, Galloway was urging the African American community to begin preparing the next generation to carry on the battle. He knew this was going to be a long-term fight, and it would be up to future generations to be prepared intellectually and, if need be, militarily. He was no doubt bolstered in this belief of the responsibility of upcoming generations by the birth of his second child, a son who would carry Abraham's name. By the end of August, Galloway had again survived numerous attempts on his life.

## A Sudden and Unexpected Departure

On September 1, 1870, Abraham Galloway suddenly and unexpectedly died. The end came so quickly that Martha Ann, who was in New Bern at the time, was unable to make it to his bedside before his death. Galloway's mother cared for him in his final hours. Though there was a general feeling that foul play was involved, Martha Ann was convinced his rheumatism as well as heart problems ultimately led to his death. News of his passing traveled quickly throughout the United States, and even his ardent foes, including the very newspapers that had denounced and ridiculed him just a day earlier, were respectful and quick to admit that he represented his people well and with the best of intentions.

His funeral at St. Paul's Episcopal Church was attended by six thousand people, still considered to be one of the largest funerals in North Carolina's history. The city's courts were closed, and flags flew at half-staff. His

Historians and forensic scientists who have studied this image believe this is a photograph of Abraham Galloway. The photograph was donated to the New Hanover County Public Library by descendants of Galloway. *Courtesy New Hanover County Public Library.*

Masonic brothers and close friends accompanied his casket, and the dozens of organizations he helped create and grow, including the black fire brigade and policemen, as well as city, county and federal officials and numerous political and fraternal organizations, lined the streets for his procession. To show his impact across racial lines, hundreds of white citizens were in attendance at his funeral, which was conducted by a white chaplain who had served in the Confederate army and then later befriended Galloway and his family.

What Abraham Galloway could have achieved if he had been born a free man will never be known. But for a man of limited education, who was never permitted the right to learn to read or write, he accomplished much. Yet as he foresaw, the Southern Democrat's fight for power would not stop with one political victory. In 1898, Southern Democrats led the only known coup d'état in America's history. With their seizure of power, the systematic oppression of African Americans began anew, and the ruling class began erasing Galloway's name from history. Even his final resting place in Pine Forest Cemetery vanished. But perhaps the greatest crime inflicted on the memory of Abraham Galloway is his near total lack of recognition. Where other men and women of far lesser achievement earned plaques, markers and statues, Galloway, a man who fought for the very traits we as Americans cherish—freedom, equality, opportunity and dignity—remains mostly unremembered. The only marker memorializing this truly heroic figure was recently erected on North Third Street, 154 years after his death.

Abraham Galloway—slave, abolitionist, Union spy, state senator, father and loving husband—was only thirty-three years old when he died.

# 8

# THE CHILDREN OF
# BULLUCK HOSPITAL

The history of Wilmington is replete with acts of violence. Some of these acts were obvious and well rehearsed: slavery, wartime occupations and the general savagery of everyday life in an eighteenth- and nineteenth-century southern seaport. Others were sudden and explosive, such as Wilmington's five great fires, each of which nearly destroyed the city, or the racial massacre of 1898, the only coup d'état in American history. But some violent acts were insidious by nature. Misfortune was able to creep into the city, unannounced, before wreaking havoc. At one time or another, malaria, smallpox, bilious fever, tuberculosis, cholera, influenza and poliomyelitis ravaged Wilmington. But of all the scourges, yellow fever was feared the most. With each outbreak, quarantines would shut down the city and port, isolating Wilmington from the rest of the world. Sometimes months would pass before the epidemic ceased. Yellow fever took the lives of thousands of Wilmingtonians.

At the dawn of the twentieth century, large commercial slaughterhouses commonly heaped butchered carcasses and eviscerations in giant piles at the rear of their properties. Household refuse was simply dumped on the outskirts of town. Many city residents kept horses, swine, cows, goats, chickens and other farm animals. There were also over seven thousand above-ground outhouses, which were poorly maintained and rarely cleaned. All of this resulting human and animal waste steadily flowed into the Cape Fear River, which, like today, was the city's only supply of fresh drinking water. Disease continued to ravage Wilmington, which ranked among the highest in the nation in per capita death rate.

The beautifully ornate entrance to the Bulluck Hospital is all that remains of the original lavish detail once found throughout the building. *Photo by John Hirchak.*

Finally, in 1911, city officials ordered all swamps in the vicinity of downtown Wilmington drained and all standing water treated to kill mosquitos, which by then were known to be responsible for malaria and yellow fever. Livestock and slaughterhouses were banned within the city limits, and all surface outhouses were ordered to be enclosed and made fly-proof. In addition to these preventative measures, the medical community helped provide better facilities to treat the sick and dying.

In 1922, Dr. Ernest S. Bulluck built an ultra-modern, four-story hospital (including the full basement) on North Front Street. Dr. Bulluck was a visionary. He introduced both the X-ray and ambulatory service to Wilmington. His was the first hospital in the state to hire a female doctor, and he reserved his entire fourth floor for the treatment of women and children, including a separate maternity room. In order to create a warm, soothing environment, which he believed led to a quicker recovery, rooms were finished with mahogany walls, Tennessee marble floors and Caen stone ceilings. Furnishings included Russian candlesticks, Arabian prayer rugs, Jacobean chairs and Rockwood vases. Though his cutting-edge practices helped advance the cause of caring for the sick, they could not stop the inevitable. Hospitals, much like battlefields, are steeped in death.

In 1944, Dr. Ernest S. Bulluck died, and the hospital officially closed its doors. The building sat vacant until 1946, when it was sold to Fleishman's Fine Clothiers. Fleishman's occupied the main floor and used the basement for storage. The upper two floors remained mostly vacant, though tenants sporadically rented individual rooms. It's from this period that the first wisps of spectral activity arise.

Though the commonality of these early occurrences are evident in hindsight, at the time, due in no small part to the fragmentary way the upper-floor units were rented, tenants didn't realize they were sharing eerily similar dreams. Their dreams always started pleasantly in some warm, open, sunlit field or park, surrounded by acquaintances. But then, inexplicably, the dreamers found they were alone, trapped in a dark, narrow maze of crisscrossing hallways, full of disorienting twists and turns. Something was giving chase—a danger, a threat—and it was very close by. But no matter how hard the dreamer tried to run, he or she became slower and slower. Corner after corner, the threat was closer, the darkness suffocating. Then, from somewhere very near, the soft, penetrating whimper of a crying child was heard. As the dreamer desperately tried to cry out, thrusting out from the darkness and grabbing at his or her clothes were the small, pale hands of a child!

At this point, most of the tenants would jump awake, screaming, flying off their beds, couches or chairs. Soaked in sweat, gasping for air, their hearts racing, the dreamers would find themselves safely back in their rooms at the old Bulluck Hospital. For most, the nightmare was over, but not for all. For a select few, when they jumped awake, they were indeed back in their rooms, but they were not alone. Standing before them was the ghost of a child. The child appeared for just a moment, perhaps a fraction of a second, before vanishing and returning to the outer realm of dreams.

In the 1990s, Fleishman's left downtown Wilmington, and the old hospital building was sold. For purposes of modernization and functionality, extensive renovation removed the once glorious interior detailing. On the upper floor, the old maternity room was rented out by a local band as a practice studio. It met several times a week, after normal business hours, and played late into the night. The band members' knowledge of the building's history was rudimentary at best.

Yet they soon discovered a special quirkiness possessed the building. On some nights, for some unexplained reason, the elevator would begin to hum as it made a slow ascent from the basement. When it reached the top floor, the doors would stutter open and light would spill into the hallway, but no one would exit. Then the doors would stutter closed, and the elevator would descend back into the bowels of the building. On other nights, the bandmates would lock up their equipment, extinguish all the lights, lock the practice studio door and then descend the stairs and exit the building. But occasionally, one of them would look up and notice all the lights on in their studio. One or two of them would race back up the stairs, unlock the studio door and, once again, turn off all the lights. Perhaps, one of the bandmates joked, it was the ghost of a child, afraid of the dark, who kept turning the lights on.

One evening, while the band was on a short break, the bass player stepped out of the practice room and into the hallway. He wasn't too surprised to find a child standing at the top of the staircase, as sometimes other business tenants had to work late and brought their children with them. But before the bass player could react, the dark-haired boy bolted down the stairs, leaving only giggles in his wake. Thinking the boy wanted to play hide-and-seek, the bass player called out, "Ready or not, here I come!" He leisurely followed the boy's giggles down the stairs to the third level. The giggles now came from a darkened room across the hallway from the staircase. The bass player jumped into the room, yelling, "Got you!"

Silence! The bass player swept his hand up and down the wall until he found the light switch. As a row of fluorescent tubes washed the room in

Bulluck Hospital (at left) and the adjoining staircase where a Wilmington police officer would often park his squad car and nap. The tunnel to the right is the only entrance to the rear of the old hospital. *Photo by John Hirchak.*

a bright, blue light, he found the room empty—not a stick of furniture, office equipment or little boy. For a moment, he was perplexed, for he was confident the boy's giggles came from that room. Then the drummer walked in behind him and said, "What are you doin'?"

The bass player had to practically peel himself off the ceiling, he jumped so high! He told the drummer what had just happened with the giggling boy playing hide-and-seek. But before the drummer could reply, the little boy giggled once more, from inside the room—and there was no place to hide.

The two bandmates jumped and screamed, then ran down the stairs and out the front door. The rest of the band, hearing the commotion, found the two on the sidewalk freaking out, swearing they would never go back inside that building. Their friends tried to calm them, but to no avail. Indeed, it was the last time the band ever practiced at Bulluck Hospital.

Perhaps the most unsettling encounter with these child ghosts takes place in the alcove at the back of the building. The alcove can be accessed only by driving through a tunnel under an adjoining building. In the alcove, off the back of Bulluck Hospital, are three original doors: a general entrance door, an ambulatory door and the door to the morgue. Many years ago, before the tunnel and alcove were lit up like an airport runway, a Wilmington police officer fell into the habit of backing his squad car down the tunnel. He would pull into the alcove and park in front of the morgue door, next to the alley weeds that once flourished beside the old exterior staircase. He would then kill the engine, lock his doors and tip his cap over his eyes, slipping into a quick ten- to fifteen-minute nap before continuing through the remainder of the graveyard shift.

When the officer would awaken, he would look out his side window at the alley weeds, which swayed slightly with the incessant breeze, and at times they appeared to be the shadowy outline of a group of anxious children. Each time, he looked carefully to assure himself they were indeed just alley weeds. Then he would tilt down the rearview mirror, brush away the sleep from his eyes, start the car and drive off. His fellow officers often chided him on the sort of special courage it took to sleep at Bulluck Hospital, where the ghosts of children loitered. But aside from some mischievous alley weeds and the occasional stray cat, he had seen neither hide nor hair of any ghosts.

Then, late one night, the officer backed his squad car down the tunnel and into the alcove. He killed the engine, locked the doors, tipped his cap and fell asleep. In what felt like a second later, he jumped awake, his head throbbing from a terrible headache. He rubbed his temples to try and soothe the pain. Glancing out the side window, he noticed the swaying alley weeds, once again deceptively looking like anxious children. He glanced at his watch and noticed he had been napping for close to twenty minutes, though it felt like a simple blink of the eyes. Feeling slightly disoriented, and with his head throbbing in pain, the officer realized he needed to get back out on patrol. As he tilted down the rearview mirror to clean the sleep out of his eyes, he sensed something was out of place. It took a moment, but then the officer saw it: nearly hidden in the dark shadows of the back seat sat a little boy, quizzically staring back at him. For a brief moment, the shocked officer and the child locked eyes. Then, after regaining his wits, the officer screamed, popped the door lock and jumped free from his car. Fumbling with his flashlight, he trained the beam into the backseat, but there was no one there.

It was the last time he ever napped at Bulluck Hospital.

# 9

# WIDOW MOORES CREEK

When news of the battles at Concord and Lexington reached Wilmington, the royal government of North Carolina collapsed. Josiah Martin, the royal governor, retreated to Fort Johnson on the Cape Fear River before taking exile on a British navy warship off the coast. Though Martin fled for his life, he, like many others in Britain, believed the rebellious southern colonies would fall back in line with a little military coaxing. He devised a plan whereby a southern Loyalist militia would establish and hold a safe route from inland North Carolina to the coast. Along this route, British troops from New England would march on Wilmington, overtake the city and then link up with an additional force to arrive by sea. These combined forces would then retake all of North Carolina before continuing south to Charleston. Martin believed this unification of southern Loyalists would quell rebellion in the lower colonies, leaving British forces free to concentrate on the northern colonies.

For years preceding the collapse of the royal government, North Carolina Patriots had been busy forming Committees of Safety to oversee local and regional government functions. Even before Martin's departure, the Patriots had been organizing a militia. So when news that a force of 1,600 Loyalist Scottish Highlanders had left Cross Creek (outside present-day Fayetteville) on February 9, 1776, the Patriots were prepared. For two weeks, the opposing forces played a game of cat and mouse, with the Loyalists attempting to get to the coast, and the Patriots blocking their every way. Adding to the Loyalists' woes was a persistent rain that carried on for most of February, chilling the air, making roads difficult to traverse and swelling the surrounding rivers, creeks and swamps.

On February 26, the Loyalist troops finally crossed the Black River, twenty-five miles north of Wilmington, and set up camp near Colvin's Creek. Six miles to the south, 150 Patriot troops under the command of Colonel Alexander Lillington arrived at the rain-swollen Widow Moores Creek (which is historically listed as non-possessive) in northwestern New Hanover County (now Pender County). Lillington quickly put his men to work on the western shore of the creek, setting up a pretend encampment and surrounding earthworks on the inside bend of a meander next to the Moores Creek Bridge. Lillington hoped this fake camp would lull the Loyalists into believing the Patriots had taken up a weak position, leaving themselves trapped in a meander with only a narrow bridge for means of retreat. Later in the day, an additional Patriot force of 850 men under Colonel Richard Caswell arrived and began building earthworks on the eastern side of the bridge. The eastern earthworks were built on a slightly elevated bluff about 150 yards up the road from the bridge and circled back around to the bank of the creek adjacent to the inside bend of the meander where the fake encampment was located. On a section of the eastern earthworks closest to the bridge, Caswell placed two small cannons named "Mother Covington and Her Daughter."

Aware of only a small, vulnerable force protecting the bridge, and convinced that if they waited another day there would be reinforcements, the Loyalists decided to lead a surprise attack. On February 27, at around one o'clock in the morning, a force of eight hundred Loyalists under the command of Lieutenant Colonel Donald McLeod departed Colvin's Creek. The Patriots already anticipated a morning attack, so several men kept the fires stoked at the fake western encampment. These men would retreat at the first sign of approaching Loyalists and warn the troops on the eastern shore. To slow the Loyalists' movement, the Patriots removed half of the planking from the bridge and greased the girders with a soft soap. When the Loyalists arrived on the western shore an hour before dusk, they discovered the abandoned camp and blazing fires.

Lieutenant Colonel McLeod was unsure whether the Patriots had quickly retreated or dropped back to a more favorable position, so he ordered his men to fan out in a line to search the woods on their march to the bridge. Two men were briefly seen on the far side of the creek, but it was unclear if they were Patriots or a part of McLeod's troops. As hundreds of Loyalists descended on the bridge, McLeod ordered men to start crossing. By boring the tips of their broadswords into the greased girders, the Highlanders crossed. The Patriots, safely hidden behind the earthworks, held their fire.

Though the Battle of Moores Creek Bridge lasted less than three minutes, it was the first Patriot victory of the American Revolution. This reconstructed bridge and surrounding earthworks are part of the Moores Creek National Battlefield. *Photo by Miles Hirchak.*

After McLeod and roughly one hundred men were gathered on the eastern shore, they proceeded to march up the road. It didn't take long for McLeod to realize he had fallen into a trap. With no other options, he shouted, "King George and broadswords!"—the signal for attack. Led by Lieutenant Colonel McLeod, the men raised their swords and charged. It would be the last broadsword charge in Highlander history.

McLeod and his men were less than sixty feet from the earthworks when "Mother Covington and Her Daughter" exploded with a deadly fusillade of musket balls and swan shot, followed by a barrage from hundreds of

Patriot muskets. The charging Loyalists were decimated. Thirty Highlanders fell dead, and another forty were wounded. Lieutenant Colonel Donald McLeod's body was shredded apart by nine musket balls and twenty-four pieces of swan shot. Leaderless and without direction, the remaining Loyalists panicked and beat a hasty retreat. Some raced into the frigid waters of the surrounding swamps, while others hastily tried to recross the bridge, slipping off the greased girders and into the racing waters of the swollen creek. Many of these men drowned or died of hypothermia, and their bodies were never recovered.

Within days of the battle, over eight hundred Loyalists involved in the march on Wilmington were arrested and held until they swore an oath never again to take up arms against the Patriots. Fifteen thousand pounds of gold coins, almost two thousand guns and rifles, a dozen wagon teams and two chests of valuable medicines were captured. When British naval forces arrived off the coast of North Carolina and learned of the Loyalist defeat, they decided to forgo invasion. These combined actions so weakened the Loyalist movement that they were never again a serious threat. For North Carolina, this meant an end to British rule forever. Wilmington and its valuable port would remain British-free and unconquered through the very end of the war.

Though the Battle of Moores Creek Bridge lasted less than three minutes, the repercussions were felt throughout Britain and the colonies. Not only was the battle the first Patriot victory of the war, but it also provided a morale boost when the rebels needed it most. Within six weeks of the victory, the North Carolina provincial congress voted to approve the Halifax Resolves, making North Carolina the first colony to declare full independence from Great Britain. The approval of the Halifax Resolves paved the way for the Continental Congress to sign the Declaration of Independence less than two months later. Finally, the failure of the British to retake North Carolina broadened the battlefield, forcing the Crown to engage Patriot troops across both the northern and southern colonies.

In the early to mid-nineteenth century, the veterans of the American Revolution were considered the "Greatest Generation." Their deeds were inspirational and sacrosanct. It's from this period that the legendary ride of Mary Slocumb was born. The power of Mary's narrative and the national fervor it created cannot be understated. Her tale had become so steeped in Revolutionary lore that the road approaching the bridge from the north, from which part of Mary's legendary ride is assigned, was renamed Slocum Trail (for reasons unknown, the final letter of her name was excluded). In 1907, a women's monument was dedicated at the site of the battle, honoring both Mary's historic ride and all women of Lower Cape Fear who sacrificed and contributed so much to the war effort. Mary and Ezekiel Slocumb's remains were disinterred from their family plot and reburied at the base of the Women's Monument. The following is a traditional account of her journey.

## MARY SLOCUMB'S LEGENDARY RIDE

Two days before the Battle of Moores Creek Bridge, Colonel Ezekiel Slocumb and a group of eighty Patriots departed Slocumb's farm, south of Mount Olive. They rode off to join Colonel Richard Caswell to assist in stopping a Loyalist militia from reaching Wilmington. Mary Slocumb remained behind to care for their infant son, Jesse. On the second evening after Ezekiel's departure, Mary dreamed she was walking through a foggy, wooded forest. Soon, she came upon a clearing and stumbled on the bodies of twenty or so dead or wounded soldiers. To the side of the group was a lone body covered in a bloodied guard cloak that she immediately recognized as that of her husband.

Mary awoke and leapt from her bed with a scream. The housemaid came rushing in, and Mary told her to watch after Jesse. Mary then saddled her horse and rode off in the direction of Wilmington. She drove her horse hard through the night. Occasionally, she would come upon other women and children, all anxiously awaiting news of their husbands' and fathers' fates. She was given directions to where Caswell's men had marched and followed the trail to Moores Creek, arriving before dawn. A thick blanket of fog soon enveloped her. She was startled by the thunderous reports of cannon and musket fire from somewhere close by. Dismounting her exhausted horse, she continued on foot in the direction of the battle, all fear quelled by her desire to see her husband. Soon, she stumbled upon a clearing where the fog had mostly lifted. To her horror, she found twenty wounded and dead soldiers, just as in her dream. As she reluctantly looked over the seemingly lifeless men, she came upon a lone body, covered near head to foot in a bloodied guard cloak, just as in her dream.

Mary cried out and fell to her knees. Choking back tears, she gingerly picked at the cloak with her trembling fingers, gently pulling the fabric free from his face. A terrible gash split his forehead wide, and a thick layer of blood and dirt covered his face, leaving him unrecognizable. She delicately

The Heroic Women's Monument at Moores Creek National Battlefield is believed to be the only monument dedicated to the sacrifices of women during the Revolutionary War. Mary and Ezekiel Slocumb's graves are in the foreground. *Courtesy of Library of Congress.*

lifted his lifeless head into her lap and began running her fingers through his hair. His body still had some warmth, meaning he must have just passed. "Oh, why could I have not ridden faster!" she wailed.

Mary rocked back and forth, and her gasping cries soon became a steady sob. Somewhere in the distance, she heard a man weakly ask for water. She remained lost in her thoughts for some time until a slight movement in her lap broke her out of her trance. It was then that she perceived the voice whispering for water was coming from her husband. Her heart pounded and her breath came fast. "Ezekiel!" she cried, as his eyes fluttered and his lips again pleaded for water.

Mary gently placed his head on the ground and ran from soldier to soldier until she came upon a canteen. Returning to her precious patient, she tenderly lifted his head into her lap. As she held the canteen to his lips so he could drink, her trembling hands caused water to splash across his face. Using the hem of her skirt, she wiped at the spilt water on his cheeks, removing some of the dried blood and dirt. As his face cleared, she realized the man she was comforting was not her husband but her neighbor, Frank Codgell.

Codgell told Mary that when he was wounded, Ezekiel gave him his guard cloak in order to keep warm. Ezekiel was unharmed and was presently chasing down routed Loyalists. Mary was so relieved to hear her husband was alive that she immediately dressed Codgell's wounds. She then went about attending to the other wounded men. A short while later, Colonel Caswell came riding up and witnessed Mary comforting these fallen warriors. He was incredibly moved by the courage and compassion she displayed. Many of the men she tended to owed their lives to this young lady.

Yet Mary's legendary ride to Moores Creek is mostly discredited. At the time of the battle, Mary would have been only fifteen and Ezekiel sixteen. Records show Ezekiel didn't even enlist until 1780. Mary herself told this story shortly before she died in 1836, at the age of seventy-six. Did she simply make up the whole event? Or could it be the simple fact that nearly sixty years had passed since that long night's ride? Many believe she simply confused the 1776 Battle of Moores Creek Bridge with the 1781 Battle of Rockfish—the two were less than ten miles apart. But whether the legendary ride of Mary Slocumb culminated at Moores Creek Bridge or Rockfish is inconsequential, especially to those wounded warriors who found comfort in her simple act of compassion. For these men, their families and their descendants, Mary Slocumb's ride is nothing short of heroic.

# 10

# THE UNUSUAL TALE OF CAPTAIN JOHN HARPER

Following Giovanni da Verrazzano's arrival off the coast of present-day Wilmington in 1524, the region was officially referred to as Cape San Romano, from which flowed the Jordan River. However, by 1600, English map makers had begun listing the region and the river as, first, Cape of Fair and then eventually, thanks in no small part to the treacherous shoals at the mouth of a river, Cape of Fear. It is on this Cape of Fear, or Cape Fear River, on Christmas Eve 1899, that Captain John Harper's voyage began.

Captain Harper piloted a steamer by the name of the *Wilmington*, a passenger, light cargo and mail ferry. The ferry typically ran daily between Wilmington and Southport, twenty miles downriver; however, an uncommon late December blizzard had kept the ship stranded at port for days. With a hold full of mail and packages, as well as a list of anxious ticketholders wishing to reach their destination by Christmas Day, Captain Harper was determined to make way. But as the *Wilmington* prepared to disembark, the engineer reported mechanical difficulties.

It was near 10:00 p.m. before the repairs were completed, and only one passenger remained aboard the ship. However, with a hold full of cargo, packages and mail, and with a slight lull in the storm, Captain Harper decided to make the journey downriver. As the *Wilmington* left the safety of its berth, the captain invited the remaining passenger, Adair McMillan, to join him on the bridge. The two men initially engaged in small talk before the conversation turned to McMillan's ties to the Cape Fear region. As the *Wilmington* slowly made its way downriver, McMillan shared a story of his great-great-grandfather Alexander Magnus McKendrick, a Scottish Highlander during the Revolutionary War.

Captain John Harper. *Courtesy of New Hanover Public Library.*

Magnus McKendrick and two other Scottish Highlanders were arrested in Wilmington by British forces in 1781. They were found guilty of treason and sentenced to death. The three condemned men were shackled, taken by barge to the western shore of the Cape Fear River and led to what was once known as the Execution Tree. The first man was stood before the tree and shot. The second suffered a similar fate. However, Magnus McKendrick was a large, strong man, and as he was being led to the tree, he turned on his captors, overpowered them and then escaped through the woods. Shortly after his escape, Magnus returned to Scotland and did not come back to

North Carolina until after the end of the war. What was most strange about the story was that after the executions in 1781, sailors on the Cape Fear River, especially late at night or during stormy weather, would occasionally report seeing an old, derelict barge drifting aimlessly with the current. On the bow of this phantom barge were the ghosts of the two Highlanders, on their knees, wrists shackled, arms raised in supplication, calling out for help. Captain Harper was familiar with the tale of the phantom barge, though he had never personally encountered this supposed ghost ship.

Then, suddenly, the conversation was interrupted when the *Wilmington* ground to a halt as it ran atop one of the river's many shifting sandbars. Save for a few bruises, the crew and ship suffered little damage. Fortunately, the tide was rising, and the captain and crew immediately went to work trying to reverse the *Wilmington* off the sandbar. The first mate, Peter Jorgensen, kept watch. With lantern in hand, Jorgensen circled the upper deck, hoping to warn approaching vessels not only of the sandbar but also of his stranded ship. After several turns around the deck, Jorgensen was startled to come upon a man precariously clinging to the outer starboard rail. The man was drenched, his long hair and beard encrusted in ice, and blood flowed from a gash across his forehead. One white-knuckled hand grasped the railing, as though he had just climbed up out of the Cape Fear and was hanging on for dear life. The other arm was stretched outright and pointing downriver. The man's pleading gaze fell on Jorgensen.

"Are you mad?" Jorgensen yelled, racing across the deck to rescue the pitiful wretch. As Jorgensen reached out to grab this stranger, the lantern light showed the man's face in full. As Jorgensen went to wrap his arms around him, the stranger vanished. Jorgensen backed away in momentary shock. After recovering, he raced off to the bridge and burst in on the captain and McMillian, shouting that he had just seen a ghost.

The captain ordered the man to calm down, accusing him of being drunk. But Jorgensen swore he had not had a drop. He quickly explained what had transpired on the upper deck, describing the man's ice-encrusted beard, the gash across his forehead and how he was pointing downriver. As the crew of the *Wilmington* worked it free of the sandbar, the captain ordered a quick search of the *Wilmington*. The captain, affected by the story he had just heard from McMillan, began to wonder if something greater was at hand.

As the crew hurriedly searched the *Wilmington*, a cry for help was heard coming off the starboard side of the ship. Knowing they were in the middle of the river and that such cries could not be heard from shore, the captain ordered the *Wilmington* starboard. As the blizzard peeled away, there before them was the rotting hulk of a wooden barge, draped in seaweed, drifting aimlessly with the river's current. On the bow knelt two men in filthy, ragged kilts, their wrists shackled, arms raised in supplication, calling out for help.

In a trembling voice the captain called for the crew to throw the men a line. Within seconds, an unraveling rope was cast from the *Wilmington* toward the pitiful men. However, when the line reached the derelict ship, it traveled through the deck and slapped against the surface of the river. The horrified crew realized they had come upon a phantom barge. Before they could react, a large swell lifted the ghost ship and drove it directly toward the *Wilmington*, but just before impact, it vanished in thin air.

The terrified crew pleaded with the captain to return to Wilmington. But since they had already passed Big Island (now called Campbell Island), the captained reasoned Southport was actually closer. The *Wilmington* was now off-center of the river and closer to the western shore, nearing Lilliput Creek just north of Orton Point. The captain was about to give orders to correct the *Wilmington*'s course when a faint cry for help was heard off the starboard side. The captain ordered silence. Again, a faint cry for help was heard. The captain immediately ordered the *Wilmington* starboard, but the frightened crew resisted. The captain quickly reminded the men that if there was someone in need of help on the river and they failed to go to their aid, not only would they all hang for murder (for that was the law of the sea), but also they would all die cowards.

The rattled crewmen regained their composure and, as the *Wilmington* turned starboard, again prepared for a rescue. As the storm buffeted, there before them was a capsized vessel. Around the vessel floated the bodies of half a dozen men. Clinging to the keel were but two survivors. With a hint of trepidation, the captain ordered the crew to throw the men a line. All hands watched in apprehension until the line slapped against the wooden hull. The two survivors were hefted aboard the *Wilmington*, and as they lifted the second man up onto the deck, the first mate, Peter Jorgensen, backed away, trembling and shouting: "You! You are the man I saw leaning from the starboard rail of this vessel no more than ten minutes ago!"

The rescued man was so weak he had to be held up by the *Wilmington*'s crew. He was shivering violently, and his beard and long hair were encrusted in ice. Blood poured from an open wound across his forehead.

"No, sir," the enfeebled man mumbled. "I have never in my life been on this river, let alone your ship."

"That can't be true!" Jorgensen shouted. "I stood before you and saw you as clear as I see you now."

The steamer *Wilmington*. *Courtesy of New Hanover Public Library.*

"This is impossible," the man replied. "We were en route from Barbados to New York when we encountered this terrible storm. As we sought the safety of your river, there was a terrible explosion aboard our ship, and I was thrown unconscious. The only reason I stand before you now is due to my friend, who held me against the keel after our ship overturned. I only regained consciousness as your ship approached. I can assure you this is the first and only time I have ever been aboard your ship."

The two near-frozen men were quickly ushered inside and treated for hypothermia. With no surviving crew to rescue, and the bodies of the dead too close to shore to retrieve, the *Wilmington* somberly made its way to Southport, arriving on Christmas morning. The two men survived their ordeal, but the strange events of that night's voyage would forever haunt the crew of the *Wilmington*. Though Captain Harper never fully understood what transpired that cold winter's eve, it's believed the crew of the *Wilmington* witnessed a rare variation of an out-of-body experience. Typically, an out-of-body experience is a first-person event; you die, see a white light and then are looking down on your own body. But in very rare cases, out-of-body experiences have been witnessed by a third party.

On Christmas Eve 1899, an explosion severely injured a man, rendering him unconscious. As his ship capsized, he was dragged into the frigid Cape Fear River, where he briefly died. His soul then appeared on the outer rail of the upper deck of the *Wilmington*, where Peter Jorgensen came upon his "ghost." Jorgensen only later realized that this "spirit" was pointing downriver, in the direction of where the wreckage and two men were ultimately found. But that is only half the wonder of this story. For the fact remains that if the *Wilmington* had been in the middle of the river, where it belonged, the crew never would have heard the cries of the second group of men. It was only from the pleas for help from the two Scottish Highlanders that the *Wilmington* was initially pulled starboard, away from mid-river, toward the western shore. If not for these Highlanders, who are forever doomed to wander the Cape Fear River, the rescued men would have undoubtedly perished.

# 11

# SCALD HEAD

Few can rival the exploits of David Fanning during the American Revolution. Though he typically rode with a force of no more than a dozen men, he fought in hundreds of skirmishes and battles, typically against superior numbers. His success can be measured in battles won, prisoners taken and weapons and supplies captured. He was severely wounded twice but never quit the fight. And though he was captured a total of fourteen times, he escaped or was released all fourteen times. He was a master recruiter and used an unbridled sense of Patriotism to help bring thousands of men into the fight. Yet despite his daring escapades and impressive success, he is not remembered as a hero.

In North Carolina, neighbor was often pitted against neighbor. Throughout the state, especially in the central portions or backcountry, the two sides were often merciless. Patriots (also known as Whigs or Rebels), and Loyalists (also known as Tories), were equally guilty of atrocities: destroying personal property, abusing and executing prisoners and murdering the innocent. And though David Fanning was simply typical in this respect, and despite his many great wartime accomplishments, he is often referred to as a monster, a demon that left death and destruction in his wake. If not for one simple fact, David Fanning would be remembered as a great warrior; streets, parks, schools and perhaps entire townships would be named in his honor. But alas, David Fanning was on the losing side of history, for he fought for the Loyalist cause.

David Fanning was born on October 25, 1755, possibly somewhere in present-day Wake County, North Carolina. From the beginning, he seemed

David "Scald Head" Fanning, escaping battle after being severely wounded. *Courtesy of the State Archives of North Carolina.*

to have a cursed childhood. Weeks before his birth, his father drowned in the Deep River. His mother struggled to raise her newborn son and his older sister, but their life of impoverishment gradually took its toll. At nine, Fanning's mother died, and he and his sister were separated. Declared a ward of the state, Fanning was placed in the negligent and abusive hands of foster parents.

While living with his foster family, Fanning contracted an acute form of porrigo, probably as a result of ringworms, commonly known as "scald head." Scald head was characterized by large, inflamed pustules that covered the head and constantly oozed pus. As the open sores became infected, they killed hair follicles, leading to irreparable hair loss. As the pus dried, the scalp took on a scaly appearance and was at times punctuated with a horrific odor. At fifteen, Fanning ran away. Two counties over, he was taken in by another family and cured of his disease. However, the damage was done, and Fanning was left with a hairless scalp that was permanently scarred and disfigured. To hide his frightful appearance, he took to always covering his head with a hat, a silk scarf or a skullcap. Later in life, his enemies derogatorily referred to him as "Scald Head" Fanning.

Though Fanning apprenticed as a loom mechanic and was a somewhat accomplished horse trainer, he turned to trading with the Catawba and Cherokee Indians. In the spring of 1775, while between tribes, Fanning was assaulted and robbed by a band of Patriots, which resulted in his becoming a radical Loyalist. He quickly lent his services to the Loyalist cause, and by December, he was actively engaged in battles and raids. In January 1776, he was captured for the first time. He was imprisoned in the jail at Ninety Six in South Carolina, shackled, stripped naked and at the very least badly mistreated. However, amnesty was soon granted to all captured Loyalists, and Fanning was released.

For the next three years, Fanning fiercely served the Crown by charging into battle, capturing Patriots, stealing horses and recruiting soldiers. Over time, Patriots came to fear him and Loyalists came to respect him. In September 1779, southern Loyalist support of the war waned, and with a fresh $300 bounty placed on his head by North Carolina state officials, Fanning decided to accept a pardon offered by South Carolina governor John Rutledge.

When Charleston fell to British forces in May 1780, Fanning eagerly became reengaged in the movement. As the war shifted southward, Fanning began heavily recruiting fellow Loyalists to serve in South Carolina's militias. When Wilmington fell in January 1781, Fanning shifted his emphasis to his old stomping ground in central North Carolina. He established a fortified base at Cox's Mill on the Deep River (near present-day Ramseur), from which, over the next year, he became the dominant force in central North Carolina. During this period, he personally led over thirty-six skirmishes and battles, capturing or killing countless Patriots, seizing or destroying vast amounts of weaponry and supplies and openly terrorizing those throughout the vast backcountry who were disloyal to the Crown. He was influential in central North Carolina's descent into a bloody civil war, where neighbor killed neighbor, burned down one another's homes, destroyed crops and livestock and committed the most vicious atrocities. In July, Major James Craig appointed Fanning a colonel and placed him in command of all Loyalist forces in the middle part of the state. In response, hundreds of Patriot forces became actively involved in the manhunt for Scald Head Fanning.

Fanning's first act as colonel was to organize and lead a brazen daylight attack on the seat of Chatham County. Fanning's men stormed the county courthouse and rescued several Loyalists who were on trial for treason. Fifty-three prisoners were taken, including court officials, militia officers and members of the general assembly. This was followed by an attack on a Patriot militia commanded by Colonel Phillip Alston at the House in the Horseshoe. The Patriots took shelter in Alston's house, which was quickly surrounded by Fanning's men. A firefight ensued in which both sides suffered casualties. Fanning's men tried to burn the Patriots out by setting a wagon filled with straw on fire and rolling it against the house. However, Alston surrendered, and the house was spared.

In August, Fanning journeyed down the Cape Fear Valley to Wilmington to resupply. During his travels to and from Wilmington, Fanning met resistance and disloyalty with merciless, brute force. It was during this bloody round-trip that Fanning was involved in an incident sometimes referred to as the "Sins of the Father." (This odd episode will be explained in the next section.) Though the Patriots of Cape Fear loathed Major James Craig and his occupying forces, for Scald Head Fanning, there was an unparalleled hatred. In the Patriots' eyes, and with total disregard for their own atrocious behavior, Fanning was accused of more bloodshed and destruction of property than any other man in the state.

Upon returning to Cox's Mill, Fanning, aided by his now infamous reputation, began a recruitment campaign that put him in command of 950 men by early September. On September 12, Fanning led a surprise attack on the temporary state capital in Hillsborough. The capital was ill prepared for such a massive, surprise assault and quickly fell. Many Loyalist prisoners were set free and over 200 enemies captured, including Governor Thomas Burke, his aides and many Patriot officers and soldiers.

The following day, the regrouped Patriot militia, under the command of General John Butler, attacked Fanning on the banks of Cane Creek, a few miles south of Hillsborough. The four-hour battle, which was one of the largest in North Carolina during the Revolutionary War, resulted in the death, wounding and capture of over 250 men. A blunder by the Loyalists' forward guard nearly led to defeat; however, Fanning quickly flanked the Patriot line and attacked Butler's troops from the rear. This surprise move forced Butler to retreat. Fanning, for a second time during the war, was seriously wounded.

While recovering from his injuries, Fanning learned of Cornwallis's defeat at Yorktown and the abandonment of Wilmington by British forces. With his supply line gone, Fanning resorted to guerrilla tactics. He negotiated several truces and pardons, but both sides repeatedly violated the agreements. The backcountry's violent civil war was in the midst of a frenzy of murder, destruction and heinous degradations.

By April 1782, it was clear the Loyalist cause was lost. Fanning married Sarah Carr, and the two newlyweds found safe passage to Charleston before sailing for St. Augustine, which was still safely under British control. In May 1783, the North Carolina General Assembly issued the Act of Pardon and Oblivion. The act was harsh in its condemnation of Loyalists; however, it did help eventually pave the way to restitution and reconciliation. But for Fanning, there would be no absolution. Only three men in the entire state were specifically excluded from pardon: Samuel Andrews, Peter Mallet and David Fanning.

When the Treaty of Paris was ratified in January 1784, Florida was returned to the Spanish and became an independent nation. Much to Benjamin Franklin's chagrin, the province of Quebec was acquired by the British. Within months, the Fannings sailed for the safety of Canada, where they remained until Fanning's death on March 14, 1825, in Digby, Nova Scotia.

# SINS OF THE FATHER

In August 1781, while Fanning was en route from Cox's Mill to Wilmington to resupply, he was informed that one of his men, a friend and fellow officer, had been murdered. The officer had ridden ahead of Fanning by one day in order to stop off and visit his wife and children. The officer rode hard all morning, and around midday, after negotiating a meandering section of road through heavily wooded swampland, he came upon a wooden bridge spanning one of the many creeks that feed into the Cape Fear River. After dismounting his horse, he dangled his legs over the bridge and went to work on a meal of cheese and bread. His horse ambled to the edge of the creek and languidly drank the tepid water. With a belly full of food, the chirping of songbirds and the rustling of leaves from a wafting breeze, the officer grew drowsy and slipped into a light nap.

He failed to hear three riders approach the bridge and dismount their steeds. It was the light shudder of footfalls on the deck boards that roused him. The officer scrambled to his feet, realizing he had foolishly left his weapons on his mount and he was all but defenseless. The three men were quickly upon him, but there was no indication of whether the men were Loyalists, Patriots, simple travelers or thieves. Before he could react or utter a greeting, one of the three men lifted a pistol and growled, "This man rides with Scald Head."

A fiery explosion of powder and lead struck the officer full on the right shoulder, throwing him backward onto the bridge decking. His horse neighed and crashed into the thick foliage of the wooded swampland. The three men stood over the officer, who raised his left arm over his head to shield the pitiless sun from his eyes. A glimmer of steel rose through the glare, high above the head of one of the strangers, and with a whoosh of air, the razor-sharp blade of a sword came slashing down on the officer's upraised hand. All five fingers were severed from the officer's hand and rained down on the blood-soaked deck. The officer begged for mercy, but none was given.

A second blow split the officer's head wide, from the top of the forehead, through the right eye and deep into the right cheek. The helpless man's deep, guttural moan was quickly drowned out by the meaty impact of steel against flesh, blow after blow, stabbing, slashing and shredding at the fallen man until there was no blood left to give.

When news of the horrific murder reached Fanning, he ordered his men into the surrounding countryside to find those who were responsible. Later that afternoon, two men were brought before Fanning, their swords and clothing steeped in blood. Fanning was stunned to discover he knew one of the men personally. The man, a supposed Loyalist, had a nearby farm and a wife who was pregnant with their first child. The man had turned either traitor or thief. Either way, Fanning withdrew his sword and ran both men through the gut, dropping them by the side of the road and leaving them to die slow, painful deaths. He and his men then rode on to the fallen officer's farm to pay their respects to the grieving family.

The brutal murder of David Fanning's friend and fellow officer. *Illustration by Jennifer Robbins.*

Early the next morning, Fanning rode to the vile traitor's farm, intent on burning the dead man's property and crops to the ground. As he approached the house and dismounted his horse, the pregnant widow emerged from the front door. Recognizing her husband's murderer, she angrily approached him. Fanning attempted to ignore the widow, but she would have nothing to do with his dismissal, accusing him of murdering an innocent man. Fanning coolly reminded the widow that it was indeed her husband who was the murderer. He told the widow how her husband had killed an unarmed man; cut off the officer's fingers on his left hand; split open his skull across the forehead, through the right eye and deep into the right cheek; and then stabbed and slashed at the body until it was nothing more than a heap of splintered flesh.

"You are a liar!" the widow shouted. "On the day you accuse him of murdering another man, he was here, on his farm, working these very fields. Nor is he the animal you make him out to be, for he could never bring such violence against another man, especially a fellow Loyalist, for my husband was faithful to both king and Crown. You, Scald Head Fanning, have murdered the wrong man, an innocent man, a decent man, and you have left me not only a widow, but you have left my soon-to-be-born child fatherless!"

Fanning, despite his typical dogged determination, was stunned. He silently retreated to his horse and rode away, leaving the widow's house and fields intact. She had no doubt struck a raw nerve when she accused Fanning of leaving her unborn child fatherless. Fanning remembered all too well the difficult path he was forced to travel in life simply because his father had drowned before he was born.

Fanning was never certain whether the widow sincerely believed her husband was a Loyalist—toiling in his fields on the day of the murder and incapable of such a heinous crime—or if she was simply trying to save her farm, for Fanning's and the widow's paths would never cross again. But the truth would reveal itself. Six weeks later, the widow gave birth to a child. Her son was born with no fingers on his left hand, and his birthmark was like a red gash that cut across his forehead, through his right eye and across his right cheek. The child was forever doomed to wear the sins of the father.

# 12

# RATTLESNAKE GRADE

On March 9, 1840, the 161-mile-long Wilmington–Weldon rail line, the longest railroad in the world owned by a single company, began service. The rail line opened inland trade routes to Wilmington, which was already the largest city and busiest port in North Carolina. In time, the railroad extended to Richmond, Virginia, and the Wilmington–Manchester line was built, extending to Charleston, South Carolina. During the Civil War, the port of Wilmington and the railroad system were the lifeline to the Confederate army. President Abraham Lincoln understood that the Union's best hope of victory was through Wilmington.

After the war, the Wilmington & Weldon Railroad Company (WWRC) continued to expand, eventually shipping freight and passengers from New Orleans to Maine. At its peak, Wilmington was home to four major lines, two minor lines and an extensive network of street railways around the port, city and beaches. The vast majority of stately mansions found in historic Wilmington come from railroad money. In 1960, the railroad's headquarters relocated to Jacksonville, Florida. Within thirty days, over five million pounds of office equipment and household goods—as well as 950 families—were removed from Wilmington, casting the city into thirty years of decline. By 1977, the valuable rails of the Wilmington–Manchester line were removed for use elsewhere, including the infamous stretch of rail known as Rattlesnake Grade.

The particular facts surrounding Rattlesnake Grade's infamy can be disputed. For example, it's unclear whether the main character's name is Charles or Joe or whether his untimely demise occurred in 1856

Mid-nineteenth-century train wrecks were typically violent and often resulted in death. *Courtesy Library of Congress.*

or 1867. But what cannot be disputed is the fact that for nearly one hundred years, thousands of people, including a then-sitting president of the United States of America, witnessed the strange phenomenon that occurred at Rattlesnake Grade. What follows is the traditional version of this story.

When the Civil War ended, Joe Baldwin, an ex-Confederate soldier with little education and few job prospects, became a vagabond. Using the southern rail system, he hopped cars, traveling from one small town to another seeking employment, but to no avail. In 1866, he arrived in Wilmington and was hired by the WWRC. He was a hard worker and quickly rose through the ranks of this growing company. In January 1867, Joe was moved from the Weldon line to the Manchester line, earning the title of conductor on the midnight mail train. A few weeks later, on a bitter, overcast February evening, Joe took the ferry from Wilmington to Eagles Island and boarded his mail train. There was no hint of the trouble to come.

Twelve miles west of Wilmington, as the train crossed Rattlesnake Creek and began a slow decline along Rattlesnake Grade, the steam whistle wailed, and the mail train stopped dead on the tracks. Joe hopped from the rear car and raced up to the locomotive. The engineer told Joe the water pump was foul and the locomotive would need to be uncoupled from the rest of the train and taken ahead for repairs. Even though no other trains were scheduled to run that night, it was not uncommon for railroads to make unannounced schedule changes or run special trains. Joe's job was to keep two lanterns burning, one on the back of the train and one on the front. When he heard the returning engineer's whistle blast, Joe was to walk up the tracks, swinging the lantern from side to side, so the engineer knew when to slow to avoid accidently bumping into the dead railcars. The engineer hoped to return within a few hours.

Joe hung a lit lantern off the rear car, and he and the mail agent, the only other person on the train, sat on the front coupling, keeping the second lantern close by. After a couple hours of idle conversation, the two men heard the faint squeal of a steam whistle. Joe grabbed the lantern, and he and the mail agent began walking up the tracks, swinging the light from side to side. A few minutes later, the whistle, now much closer, screeched again. The two men froze. The train was coming from behind them! Joe handed the mail agent the lantern and told him to run up the tracks, just in case, unsure if their locomotive was also returning. Joe then took off running to the back of the train to grab the second lantern.

As Joe raced along the cars, the steam whistle howled again. The oncoming train was close and traveling fast. Reaching the rear car, he grabbed the handrail and swung up the back steps. He could feel the car shaking violently as the approaching train rounded the bend at an alarming speed. Joe snatched the lantern off its hook and turned just in time to face the oncoming menace. The charging engine smashed into the back of the mail train in an explosion of metal, wood, steam, blood and flesh.

Over the coming days, cleanup crews picked through the massive debris field. Mutilated engine and car parts littered the tracks, woods and swamp. Though his body was torn apart and scattered, most of Joe Baldwin's remains were found. The only part missing was his head. They searched the surrounding swamp, convinced it had flown into the murky water, but it was never found.

By 1873, mail train engineers had begun reporting strange lights on the tracks near Rattlesnake Grade. At first, there were two lights, known briefly as the "rattlesnake eyes." However, after an earthquake in 1886, one light vanished. The single light at Rattlesnake Grade was reported to be the size of a lantern, slowly swinging back and forth a few feet above the tracks. Those who saw it claimed it was the ghost of Joe Baldwin looking for his missing head.

The issue of the light wreaked havoc on night trains traveling through Rattlesnake Grade. Each time an engineer witnessed the swinging light, he

The small figurine of headless Joe Baldwin, with lantern aglow, can be found at the Wilmington Railroad Museum in downtown Wilmington. *Photo by John Hirchak.*

was forced to slow his train to a crawl for fear there was an actual stopped train on the tracks. To resolve this issue of the Wilmington–Manchester line, it soon became custom to swing two lanterns instead of one. In 1889, President Grover Cleveland visited Wilmington. When the presidential train was preparing to depart for Charleston, the president noticed the brakeman waving two lanterns. He asked the man why he swung two lamps instead of the customary one. The president was told it was because Joe Baldwin had still not found his head. As they approached Rattlesnake Grade, President Cleveland kept a keen eye out and later stated he had personally seen Joe Baldwin's light.

Around 1890, the crossroads at Rattlesnake Grade (which was then known as Farmer's Turnout) was settled and renamed Maraco, which the locals soon shortened to Maco. The legend of Joe Baldwin's light soon became known as the "Maco light." By the 1900s, traveling to see the light was a rite of passage. Scores of people would journey out to Maco, park their cars and walk the tracks up the old Rattlesnake Grade, where Joe Baldwin had been decapitated. Though some claimed to see nothing, others saw a light flaring in the distance, three feet above the left rail, gently swinging back and forth. The light would typically travel from east to west, toward the observer, and then stop. It was strong enough to glimmer brightly off the left rail, but there was never a body in tow. The light would then slowly recede and vanish into the inky blackness.

The legend of the Maco light continued to grow, and for a while it became a national sensation. In 1957, *Life* magazine ran a piece on the phenomenon. In 1964, the famous ghost hunter Hans Holzer was hired to investigate the strange light. Some of America's best and brightest, from Camp Lejeune, Fort Bragg and other nearby military bases, traveled to Maco in a show of bravado. Though many of these brave soldiers deny it, they, like others who witnessed the Maco light, were frightened. A few hardy, often intoxicated souls, however, would charge the light, only to see it snuff out when they were within a few yards and then suddenly reappear behind them.

When the rail lines were removed in 1977, the Maco light ceased to be. Some say Joe was confused over the loss of the rail line he faithfully walked for one hundred years. Others say he was angry at the abandonment of the line and was off sulking. And still others say he simply tired of looking for his head and decided it was time to move on. But for some, the ghost of Joe Baldwin never really went away.

The last vestige of Wilmington's once thriving railroad community can still be found at the Railroad Museum, near where the old switchback was located along the Cape Fear River. Inside the museum are several magnificent, well-detailed model train lines depicting old Wilmington's rich railroad history. On one stretch, the miniature train runs past a small forest of long-leaf pines, open farmland and a few cows, through a swamp and over a creek before whizzing past a seemingly benign figurine. An astute observer will notice the tiny, headless figure is waving a lantern. This is all that remains of the vagabond Joe Baldwin.

# 13

# THE BOY FROM HAMBURG

William Ellerbrook was born in 1856 to a caring, loving family. He was raised along the river Elbe, in the free, sovereign state of Hamburg, seventy-five miles south of Denmark. Despite northern Europe's ongoing political unrest, William spent much of his childhood playing with friends along the vibrant Hamburg riverfront, which at the time was home to Europe's largest port. However, by William's fourteenth birthday, Hamburg had been absorbed into the new German Empire. With near daily protests and threats of warfare, William's parents quietly scrimped and saved until they had enough money to purchase a single, one-way steerage passage ticket aboard a Hamburg-America Line steamer.

To William, the news of his departure was sudden and surprising. On the brisk walk to the steamer, William's parents explained to their distraught son that he was going to live with and be raised by his uncle in an American seaport called Wilmington. The future of Hamburg, Germany, and greater Europe, was uncertain, they told William, and this passage was the one final gift they could impart on him. William pleaded with his parents not to be sent away, but they were adamant. At the base of the steamer's gangplank, William's mother trembled and wept as she hugged him goodbye. Then his father, no longer able to feign stoicism, grabbed his child in his arms.

"It pains us to send you away," William's father sobbed, "but Hamburg has become a dangerous place, and your mother and I need you to go to America. I know it is difficult to understand, but sometimes parents have to be willing to give up their child in order to keep their child safe. One day, you will have your own family, and you will discover the same amount of love for your child as we have for you. Maybe then you will understand why we did this and you will forgive us."

William cried as he was ushered up the gangplank by a crewman. His parents promised they would write often and assured him they would soon follow him to America. But William would never see his parents again.

The two-week voyage was miserable. Steerage passage was the lowest deck of the ship, and the dank confines were overcrowded and offered no privacy. William was surrounded by complete strangers, many of whom spoke little German. He was so homesick for his family and friends that he could not eat. By the time he arrived in Wilmington, he was so week that his uncle, Henry Theodore Lemmerman, had to carry the boy off the ship.

William's first few weeks in America were just as depressing. He found himself a foreigner in a foreign land. Everything about the sultry southern city was unfamiliar. He spoke little to no English, so even the simplest interaction was a chore. Though there was a sizeable German population in the city, William grew so reclusive that he made no friends. As his homesickness deepened, William's uncle realized he needed to intervene.

Early one morning, Uncle Henry roused William from his sleep. He told the boy to get dressed and to come downstairs for breakfast. It was still dark outside when a forlorn William drew up a chair at the table. There his uncle informed the boy that to help him adjust to his new life in America, he was to be given two new responsibilities. The first was an apprenticeship aboard the tug his uncle captained. Uncle Henry told William he understood how the boy loved and missed the river Elbe, but he assured his nephew that the Cape Fear River was just as hypnotic and captivating and, given enough exposure, would grow on him like home.

William nodded that he understood what his uncle was asking of him. He, too, wanted to feel something besides longing. He also came to realize, in the short time he had been in Wilmington, that his uncle truly had his best interests at heart. After a few introspective moments, William said, "Uncle Henry, you said I'd have two new responsibilities. What is the second one?"

"Ah, nephew, you will find out soon enough."

William didn't utter a word as he and his uncle descended Princess Street toward the riverfront. William was trying hard to figure out what his second responsibility would be. As they walked, William spotted a hint of dawn beginning to shelter the evening stars. The familiar sounds and smells of a river port wafted through the air as the two stopped beside his uncle's tug. Through the incessant cawing of the seagulls, William could hear a distinct, high-pitched yelp. Lost in thought, it took William a moment to realize his uncle was staring at him.

"William," Uncle Henry sighed, "I left Hamburg on my journey to America before you were born. But I still remember how I felt leaving behind my home, my family and my friends." Uncle Henry's gaze dropped as he reflected on his long walk up the gangplank. "I guess what I want you to know is that my home is now your home, and while I can't replace your parents, we are family and I will take care of you as though you are my own son. So that takes care of two of the three things you probably miss the most."

William gave his uncle a slight smile.

"Now, regarding your friends," Uncle Henry paused. "Well, let's just say I'm too old to be your friend. However, I may have a solution to this problem, at least for the short haul."

William looked at his uncle questioningly.

"Your second responsibility is on my boat," Uncle Henry continued, nodding toward the tug. "I promise that if you take care of this responsibility, she will remain your friend for life."

It suddenly occurred to William that the intermittent yelping sound he kept hearing was coming from the deck of the tug. Uncle Henry nodded, indicating it was OK for William to step onto the boat. William cautiously climbed over the gunwale and onto the slightly pitching main deck. There, he discovered a yawping puppy tied off to the winch. The puppy was so tiny that she couldn't have been more than four or five weeks old. She possessed no discernible traits or markings of any breed—she was a true mutt. As William approached, the little dog began yapping louder and jumping against the rope that restrained her, pumping her tail back and forth at a rate that seemed physically impossible. William knelt beside the dog, allowing her to jump into his arms and excitedly lick his face and neck. As the hyperactive dog squirmed, Uncle Henry approached the two from behind, placing one hand on William's shoulder while the other scratched the puppy's head. For the first time since leaving Hamburg, William didn't feel so utterly alone.

As the days passed, William was unable to settle on a name for the puppy, so he simply called her "Dog." William quickly adapted to his new responsibilities and his new family, and he truly enjoyed the long days spent with his uncle and the dog aboard the small tug. Uncle Henry found the puppy incredibly amusing, and though the tug didn't have a stern cabin—and therefore no stern roof, or "poop deck"—he would belly laugh every time the dog defecated on the aft main deck. "William," he would guffaw from the wheelhouse, "it's time to make your way to the poop deck."

As the days turned into weeks, the three fell into a comfortable routine. William and his uncle would laugh hysterically as the quickly growing, clumsy dog would gallop in circles around the wheelhouse, barking at all the seagulls that came to rest atop the tug's gunwale. As the yapping dog approached, the seagulls would open their wings and drift a few feet up off the gunwale until the dog passed, and then they'd drift back down to await her next lap. So for the excitable dog, it was like a never-ending journey.

Over time, the dog discovered her coordination and timing, and she learned to lunge upward at the slower-moving seagulls. Though she never caught one, she did learn a valuable lesson: if you jump too high and clear the gunwale, you end up in the river with a snout full of water, paddling with all your might just to stay afloat. On these occasions, Uncle Henry would laugh hysterically as he swung the tug around. William, with boat hook in hand, would snag the dog by her rope collar and drop her back on deck. Then, after a brief respite, she would continue on her patrol around the wheelhouse.

As the weeks turned into months, William and the dog became inseparable. One afternoon, while chugging upriver back to port, Uncle Henry caught a glimpse of William as he neatly coiled the thick rope hawsers on the aft deck. The dog sat attentively by his nephew's side, and after each coil William made with the hawser, he would reach out and scratch the dog on the forehead, and the dog would reply with a quick lick of William's hand. So after tying off at port, as the two walked up Princess Street back to their home off Blount's Alley, Uncle Henry asked the boy why he still called the dog "Dog."

"I guess I never quite thought of a name that really fit her," William answered.

"Well she's your dog," Uncle Henry said, "and you're entitled to call her what you like. But seeing as she can't name herself, and being pretty certain if she could, she wouldn't call herself 'Dog,' I think it's time you gave her a proper name."

The three stopped, and William looked warmly at the dog. As had become her habit, she immediately worked her snout into William's hand, forcing him to pet her. As William stooped over and began to stroke the dog's neck, he gave it some more thought. But after a few minutes, William let out a long sigh and stood back upright.

"I don't know, Uncle Henry. It should probably be something special, but nothing sounds right. What do you think?"

Uncle Henry thought about it for a moment as he watched the dog work her snout back into William's hand again and again, until he finally began to pet her.

"Well, it's obvious this dog has become the boss of your hand, and I have no doubt she is the boss of your heart, so I think you should call her 'Boss.'"

"Boss," William whispered to the dog, allowing the name to linger in the air. "Boss," he said again, as her tail began to pump wildly back and forth. "I think she likes it."

## Boss and the Captain

As the months turned into years, William completed his apprenticeship aboard his uncle's tug, and he, too, became a captain. Over the years, William learned to read and write English, and with each passing day, Wilmington felt more and more like home. He still missed his family and friends in Hamburg, but the occasional letter would suffice. With the aid of the congenial Boss, William made many acquaintances and developed many new friendships. He also developed a strong sense of decency and compassion, and when a call for help was issued—be it fire, flood or fundraiser—William was quick to volunteer.

As his uncle had assured William eight years earlier, with Boss by his side, William would never want for friendship. Whether on ship or shore, Boss and the captain were always in each other's company. Most Wilmingtonians knew William through Boss and couldn't imagine one without the other. Many joked that the two were co-joined by some invisible bond. When in town, shopkeepers would call the two over for a few kind words for Captain William Ellerbrook and a special treat for Boss—from Mr. Rush, the grocer, a piece of cheese or meat; from Mr. Gilbert, the baker, a spare biscuit; from Mr. Ahrens, the warehouse owner, a cup of cool water; and from Mr. Peck, the hardware dealer, the occasional kerchief as a collar. Over time, Captain Ellerbrook and Boss had endeared themselves to the people of Wilmington.

## Fire on Front

It was just after midnight on Sunday morning, April 11, 1880, when Boss heard the distant clanging of the fire bell. Her whining and pacing roused William, who jumped from bed and quickly got dressed. Whenever the fire bell rang, William raced to the wharves to see if his tug was needed to rescue people or stock or for towage. As William and Boss raced down Princess Street, they could

The northeast corner of Dock and Front Streets as it appears today. In April 1880, a grocer operated out of the first floor, and to the left of the grocery was George Peck's hardware store. *Photo by John Hirchak.*

smell the acrid smoke drifting inland, but when they reached the intersection of Princess and Front Streets, they realized the fire was not at the wharves but two blocks south, along Front and Dock Streets.

The fire had started in Mr. Ahrens's grain and hay warehouse on Dock Street, and by the time William and Boss arrived, the building was engulfed in flames. The fire quickly spread to Antoine Rush's grocery, on the corner of Dock and Front Streets. Mr. and Mrs. Solomon, who lived above the grocery, barely escaped the conflagration with their lives. Soon, George Peck's adjoining hardware store had smoke billowing from the second-floor windows, as did David Gilbert's bakery. As the firemen fought the blaze, a dozen men rushed into George Peck's store in an attempt to remove the highly flammable jugs of turpentine and barrels of gunpowder.

The only warning that the western wall of the Ahrens' warehouse was about to collapse was a rapid series of pops followed by a low, guttural rumbling.

Someone in the hardware store screamed, "Get out!" just before the massive wall of brick and mortar came crashing down. The men inside ran for the door just as the collapsing wall sent a billowing wave of smoke and ash tumbling out onto Front Street. Firefighters quickly rushed to the remnants of the hardware store and began pulling men from the wreckage. All the men were injured to varying degrees, including three of William's friends: Charlie Burkhimer, Charles Myers and Frank Meier. Though several of the men were knocked unconscious from falling debris, all the men were accounted for, and no lives were lost. Shortly thereafter, the fire was brought under control.

## THE HEROIC DOG

Uncle Henry woke early Sunday morning and found the neighborhood abuzz with news of the terrible fire that took place overnight. During breakfast, he read the newspaper's morning edition, chronicling the destructive blaze. As he perused the list of those hurt in the fire, he was relieved to read that most of the injuries were non–life threatening. Though some of the men's injuries were severe, all were expected to make a full recovery. Though the paper referred to many heroic deeds that took place during the blaze, no specifics were given.

It wasn't until after breakfast that Uncle Henry began to realize William was absent. Though it was Sunday, a day of rest, William usually awoke early, typically at Boss's urging, and rarely slept through breakfast. Uncle Henry decided to check in on William but found his room empty and the bed unmade. Though it was unlike William to leave the house unannounced, Uncle Henry rightly assumed the boy had awakened to the clanging of the fire bells and went to see if he could be of assistance. After eight years as his nephew's guardian, Uncle Henry felt the anxiousness of a father. He decided to take a stroll into town to search for William and Boss.

His first stop was at the ruins of the fire, where a throng of onlookers gawked at the destruction, which was indeed vast. The fire chief, a friend of William's, told Uncle Henry that he had indeed seen William and Boss at some point during or just after the fire, but with all the chaos, he didn't notice when they left. He was positive that William was not amongst the injured men, who were all accounted for and were being cared for throughout town. More than likely, he told Henry, William and Boss were helping comfort one of their injured friends.

Uncle Henry's next stop was at the wharf where William's tug was tied off. However, when he arrived, he found no sign of either William or Boss. Again, feeling the anxiousness of a father, Uncle Henry returned to the ruins and asked the fire chief if he and his men could do a quick search of the rubble, just to put an old man's mind at ease.

Within a matter of minutes, a foot was found protruding from the rubble of the burned-out hardware store, less than eight feet from the doorway. The gathering crowd grew tense as the firemen began removing chunks of scorched brickwork from atop the body. Uncle Henry was frantic and pleaded with the firefighters to assure him it was not William, but the little they could see of the body was burned beyond recognition. As the men worked to untangle the debris, the fire chief confidently assured Uncle Henry that it couldn't have been William, for he was almost positive he had seen him after the fire was brought under control.

After several agonizing minutes, much of the immolated body was exposed, but the chief couldn't tell if the victim was a man or a woman. Even after the back of the blackened, hairless head was exposed, the face, which looked to be burned to the skull, remained buried facedown in several inches of wet ash. One of the victim's arms was stretched forward, above the head, in the direction of the doorway, and a fireman began to clear the debris from over it. Suddenly, they all stopped. Several of the hardened firefighters gasped, and one or two began to weep. Curled up beside the scorched arm, with her snout buried beneath the hand, were the charred remains of Boss.

Uncle Henry collapsed in grief and was helped to a stoop across the street. Most of people in the growing crowd began to cry as the weeping firemen gently lifted William's and Boss's remains from the ash. The men delicately placed the bodies on the sidewalk, but before they could be covered, a woman in the crowd cried out that there was something protruding from Boss's mouth. The fire chief went down on one knee and gently parted Boss's jaw, freeing a piece of her master's peacoat. Then, the chief, fully understanding what had taken place in that burning building, buried his face in his hands and began sobbing.

The final few moments inside the hardware store just prior to the wall's collapse had been chaotic. Between the cover of darkness and the blinding smoke, it had been difficult to see inside of the building, let alone know who was in there. As the wall began to come down, the men inside the building had poured out of the hardware store's doorway. The great billow of smoke, heat and debris that had followed made it impossible to see. The injured men had been quickly rushed from the

Captain William Ellerbrook and Boss's monument at Oakdale Cemetery, erected by the people of Wilmington. *Photo by John Hirchak.*

scene and taken to different locations to be treated. However, William Ellerbrook's legs had been crushed by the falling wall, and he had been knocked unconscious. Only Boss, who had remained uninjured, knew William was still inside the building.

Boss had grabbed William's pea coat and tried to pull him free, but the weight on his legs and her diminutive size worked against her. She kept tugging on his coat until a piece of it tore off in her mouth. Then, as the hair on her back literally burned off, rather than run out to save herself, Boss had curled up beside William's outstretched arm and then, as she was known to do, nudged her snout under William's hand. Boss had given the final few moments of her life comforting her friend.

When news of William Ellerbrook's and Boss's deaths spread, the entire city became consumed with grief over the tragedy. Not only were people saddened by the loss of such a young man, for William Ellerbrook was only twenty-four years of age, but they were also deeply moved by the heroic dog that gave her life to comfort her family. A makeshift memorial was set up at the ruins of the fire, where flowers were placed and notes of sorrow were left. Flags throughout the city—including the customhouse, the German imperial consulate, the area firehouses and all ships in port—were lowered to half-mast. The wheelhouse of Captain Ellerbrook's tug was draped in black, as was his uncle's home.

On the day of the funeral, an overflow crowd gathered at St. Paul's Lutheran Church, where William had been a member. Inside the church, before the altar, Captain William Ellerbrook's coffin was placed on a tuft of flowers. Beside his coffin was placed a smaller, specially built casket containing Boss. Following the service, the two caskets were led to Oakdale Cemetery, where they were buried side by side, just as they were in life.

The people of Wilmington were so incredibly moved by this tragic loss that they began raising money in order to erect a monument atop their graves. If you visit Oakdale Cemetery today, you can stop by the front office, and they will give you a map so you can find the monument. Many people still

The stone carving of Boss as it appears on the back of the monument at Oakdale Cemetery.

visit the grave, so enduring and endearing is the story. Most people simply read the front of the monument, the life and death details of Captain William Ellerbrook, before moving on to other notable grave sites and interesting headstones. However, if you do visit their grave, don't make the same mistake, for on the back of the monument, the people of Wilmington left a special gift for a very heroic dog. On the back of the monument is etched an image of Boss. Above her are the words: "Faithful Unto Death."

# BIBLIOGRAPHY

Cape Fear Historical Institute. "Colonel Bludworth's Hollow Cape Fear Citadel." http://www.cfhi.net/ColonelBludworthsHollowCapeFearCitadel.php.

Capps, Michael A. *Moores Creek National Battlefield—Administrative History.* Washington, D.C.: Government Printing Office, 1999.

Cashman, Diane Cobb. *Cape Fear Adventure: An Illustrated History of Wilmington.* Woodland Hills, CA: Windsor Publications, 1982.

Cecelski, David S. *The Fire of Freedom: Abraham Galloway and the Slaves' Civil War.* Chapel Hill: University of North Carolina Press, 2012.

Cecelski, David S., and Timothy B. Tyson. *Democracy Betrayed: The Wilmington Race Riot of 1898 and Its Legacy.* Chapel Hill: University of North Carolina Press, 1998.

Curtis, Edward E. *The Organization of the British Army in the American Revolution.* New Haven, CT: Yale University Press, 1926.

Eastman, Tamara J., and Constance Bond. *The Pirate Trial of Anne Bonny and Mary Read.* Cambria, CA: Fern Canyon Press, 2000.

Ellet, Elizabeth F. *The Women of the American Revolution.* New York: Baker and Scribner, 1849.

Fanning, David. *The Narrative of Colonel David Fanning.* Richmond, VA: J.H. Wheeler, 1861.

Fonvielle, Chris E., Jr. *Fort Anderson: Battle for Wilmington.* Cambridge, MA: Da Capo Press, 1999.

Hall, Lewis Philip. *Land of the Golden River.* Vol. 1, *Old Times on the Seacoast, 1526 to 1970.* Wilmington, NC: privately printed, 1975.

———. *Land of the Golden River*. Vol. 2, *This Fair Land of Ours*, and Vol. 3, *Old Wilmington and the Greater in Its March to the Sea*, Wilmington, NC: privately printed, 1980.

Hoffman, Glenn. *Building A Great Railroad: A History of the Atlantic Coast Line Railroad Company*. N.p.: CSX Corporation, 1998.

Lawson, John. *New Voyage to Carolina*. London: privately printed, 1709.

Lee, Lawrence. *The Lower Cape Fear in Colonial Days*. Chapel Hill: University of North Carolina Press, 1965.

Lee, Robert E. *Blackbeard the Pirate: A Reappraisal of His Life and Times*. Winston-Salem, NC: John F. Blair, 1974.

Lennon, Donald R., and Ida B. Kellam. *The Wilmington Town Book*. Raleigh: North Carolina State Archives, 1973.

Matthews, Marty. "House in the Horseshoe: David Fanning Bio." NC Historic Sites. http://www.nchistoricsites.org/horsesho/dfanning.htm.

McKoy, Henry Bacon. *Wilmington, N.C.—Do You Remember When?* Greenville, SC: privately printed, 1957.

Moore, Louis T. *Stories Old and New of the Cape Fear Region*. Wilmington, NC: Wilmington Printing Company, 1956.

Noffke, Jonathan. *The Civil War Years at the Bellamy Mansion*. Brochure available at Bellamy Mansion. March 1995.

Pickering, David. *Pirates: From Blackbeard to Walking the Plank*. New York: Harper Collins, 2006.

Preik, Brooks Newton. *Haunted Wilmington and the Cape Fear Coast*. Wilmington, NC: Banks Channel Books, 1995.

Reaves Collection. New Hanover County Public Library.

Reaves, William M. *Strength Through Struggle: The Chronological and Historical Record of the African-American Community in Wilmington, North Carolina, 1865–1950*. Wilmington, NC: New Hanover Public Library, 1998.

Shingleton, Royce. *High Seas Confederate: The Life and Times of John Newland Maffitt*. Columbia: University of South Carolina Press, 1994.

Sprunt, James. *Chronicles of the Cape Fear River, 1660–1916*. Raleigh, NC: Edwards & Broughton, 1916. Reprint, Wilmington, NC: Broadfoot, 1992.

———. *Tales and Traditions of the Lower Cape Fear, 1661–1896*. Wilmington, NC: Legwin Brothers Printers, 1896. Reprint, Spartanburg, SC: The Reprint Company, 1973.

Steelmen, Ben, and Leslie Gruber. *Wilmington at the Millennium*. Wilmington, NC: Wilmington Star News, 2000.

Stephens, John Richards. *Captured by Pirates*. Cambria Pines by the Sea, CA: Fern Canyon Press, 1996.

Tetterton, Beverly. *Wilmington—Lost but Not Forgotten.* Wilmington, NC: Dram Tree Books, 2005.

Turberg, Edward F., and Martin, Christopher. *Historic Architecture of New Hanover County, North Carolina.* Wilmington, NC: New Hanover County Planning Department, 1986.

Wessex Archaeology, Ltd. "The Bottle Wreck (Site 5013)." http://www.wessexarch.co.uk/projects/marine/alsf/wrecks_seabed/round2/5013/index.html.

Wrenn, Tony P. *Wilmington, North Carolina: An Architectural and Historical Portrait.* Charlottesville: University of Virginia Press, 1984.

*Wrightsville Beach Magazine.* "Blockade Runners: The Ships, the Captain, the Sword." January 2001.

# ABOUT THE AUTHOR

J ohn Hirchak lives with his wife, Kim, and their son, Miles, in Wilmington, North Carolina. He is the author of *Ghosts of Old Wilmington*, and his short stories and poetry have appeared in small press magazines, including *Aldebaran*, *Calliope* and *Encore*. In 1999, John and Kim created the Ghost Walk of Old Wilmington, followed by the Haunted Pub Crawl and the Hollywood Location Walk. They also own the Black Cat Shoppe and Jokilimi Island Imports.